MW00637883

Corrections in California:
An Introduction
to
Probation, Institutions,
and Parole

2nd Edition

by

Edward E. Peoples, DPA
Instructor Emeritus
Administration of Justice Department
Santa Rosa Junior College

Published by **Meadow Crest Publishing on CreateSpace**

Meadow Crest Publishing
P. O. Box 1485, Forestville, CA 95436
Phone: **(707) 887-1877.** e-mail: Meadowcrestpublishing@msn.com

Brief Table of Contents

Preface

The nature and scope of this text is reflected in one word of the title, ***Introduction***. This is an introduction to the justice system's formal responses to crime and public safety within the field of corrections. The term corrections needs clarification. To some, the word *corrections* refers to custodial institutions such as jails and prisons. Perhaps that is because many of those who staff these institutions hold the job title of correctional officers and are visible to the general public. To others, the term *corrections* refers to adult corrections. This text takes the position that both of these views narrow the field of study too much for one to appreciate the full range of agencies, efforts, and functions served by the various sub-systems within the broad corrections field.

Correctional efforts and functions at the adult level begin after conviction (with two exceptions); after an offender has been processed by law enforcement and the courts. These efforts and functions are provided by probation officers, jail and state institutional correctional officers and counselors, and parole agents. At the juvenile level, correctional efforts begin even before a court process is initiated and continues through and far beyond what occurs in juvenile court, and includes institutions and parole.

This text introduces the reader to those three components of the correctional process: probation, institutions, and parole. As indicated, it examines both adult and juvenile corrections. Material on federal corrections is not included in this text, except for a few photos and comments on Alcatraz prison. Finding the proper sequence in presenting the material was a challenge. Ultimately it will depend on how an instructor might cover the material in a course and whether an instructor even includes information on juvenile corrections in the same course with adult corrections. The sequence presented in this text mixes the content, hopefully, to achieve some semblance of continuity. Any one instructor might well alter this mixture in his or her course presentation.

There are certain significant differences between adult and juvenile corrections and between how offenders are treated, and yet there are many similarities. Adult probation officers serve as the investigative and enforcement arms of the court, and enforce the orders of the court while at the same time helping the offender change his or her behavior. The efforts of parole are similar in nature but at a different level of government and with a different clientele.

ii

County jails are designed to hold individuals in custody pending trial, or other proceedings, and those serving misdemeanor sentences. Juvenile halls provide similar services.

The purpose of adult institutions is punishment, although in July 2005, Governor Schwarzenegger added the term *Rehabilitation* to the title of the Department of Corrections.

At the juvenile level, probation also represents the investigative and enforcement arms of the court. However, juvenile court and probation are blended together more in effort and structure than their adult counterparts. Theoretically, juvenile institutions offer the custody of a closed institution, but with a broad overlay of rehabilitation programs for young offenders. Parole serves as an extension of those efforts.

Another difference between adult and juvenile procedures is how offenses are categorized. Adults commit either misdemeanors or felonies, but both are **crimes**. Technically speaking, juveniles do not commit crimes. Juvenile offenses are divided into two categories: (1) status offenses, which are not really law violations, but represent behaviors in which juveniles are prohibited from engaging in because of their age status, such as being a runaway, an incorrigible, or a school truant; and (2) law violations, which include those offenses that would be crimes if committed by adults.

There was a time when there was not only a theoretical, but a practical difference between adult and juvenile offenders. Adults committed crimes, were responsible for their acts, and were punished. Juveniles committed offenses (not crimes), were less than fully responsible, and were counseled and treated. The terminology still reflects much of those differences but often today there is little difference between correctional practices, and protection of the public is the primary goal of each.

Until certain legislative and administrative changes were made in 2011 and 2012, there were clear distinctions made between probation and parole, and jail and prison. Probation was granted to a convicted offender in lieu of receiving and/or serving a sentence. Jail was a facility at the county level used to detain suspects pending trial or to house those serving misdemeanor sentences or serving time as a condition of probation, and prison was a facility at the state level used to house convicted felons serving a sentence. Current legislation and state administrative policies are blurring these distinctions and changing these definitions. These changes were triggered by **A.B. 109**, effective October 1, 2011. The changes seem to be money driven. They will affect felony sentencing, county jail populations and credit time, and post-release supervision and parole.

Certain classifications of felons now serving state time are being returned to county jurisdictions to serve their time in jail, and certain so-called *low risk* convicted felons are sentenced to serve their time in local jails instead of prisons. I expect that the time will come soon when many of those released from prison on parole will instead be returned to court for an order of conditional release on probation, thereby reducing parole caseloads and personnel, saving the state a substantial amount of money.

Chapter 1 offers an overview of how probation developed in California leading to the practices of today. **Chapter 2** describes the full array of services provided by adult probation during the pre-trial and sentencing proceedings.

Chapter 3 details adult probation supervision, and includes a section on county parole, as provided by deputy probation officers. **Chapter 4** summarizes the custody and control services found within the county jail.

Chapter 5 continues the presentation of material at the adult level by offering a general history of prison development, highlighting the principles and concepts that shaped prison development in California. It includes photos of selected state and federal institutions.

Chapter 6 focuses on the California Department of Corrections and Rehabilitation: its history and construction of the initial prison system. Photos of selected prisons within California are included.

Chapter 7 examines the processes that occur within CDCR's adult prison system, including inmate classification and placement, and the roles and responsibilities of correctional officers.

Chapter 8 shifts the material back to the juvenile level, with an overview of how and why our juvenile probation system developed, and includes a detailed description of how juvenile court and probation treat status offenders and juvenile law violators. This chapter also includes a review of the nature and purpose of juvenile halls.

iv

Chapter 9 focuses entirely on the Division of Juvenile Facilities, formerly named the California Youth Authority, and details the roles, processes and functions in the state's institutional system. **However, by 2014, the state plans to cease operating juvenile justice agencies and will transfer all responsibilities having to do with juveniles over to local county courts.**

Chapter 10 describes state parole, and is divided into two sections: adult parole and juvenile parole. In California today, one agency is responsible for the parole processes for both adults and juveniles, the Board of Parole Hearings.

There are approximately forty photographs in the text, included primarily in those chapters that examine the institutional aspects of corrections. Most of the photos were either taken by or collected by this author over a period of some 35 years. The quality of the photos varies, primarily because of the dates they were taken and the exposures available at the time. Some were taken from the CDCR website.

Also included are job descriptions, employment training, and employment opportunities for local jail correctional officers, juvenile hall youth corrections officers, state youth and adult correctional officers, county probation officers, and state parole agents. Academy training and job certification for all local correctional staff is provided through the State Board of Corrections. State youth and adult corrections officers usually receive their training at the state academy located in Galt.

The text was written with the needs of the student as primary. It offers an introduction to corrections for the entry level college student in a readable style that is interesting and current, and is published and bound in a manner to keep the cost as low as reasonably possible. Each chapter begins with a list of key terms and concepts to guide the student's study, and these terms and concepts are bolded wherever they occur in the chapters.

Some of the material on adult probation and jail custody services are condensed versions of similar material from the author's text, *Criminal Procedures in California*, and some of the material on juvenile court and probation is a condensation of material from the author's text, *Juvenile Procedures in California*.

Table of Contents

Chapter 1: Probation History - Concepts and Practices

Key Terms and Concepts

Common Law	*Killets* case
Determinate Sentence Law	Probation
Disparity	Probation subsidy
John Augustus	Recognizance

Introduction

Probation entered the American criminal justice system during the mid-1800s as a legal device to provide relief from the harsh penal sanctions of the day. Through the 1700s, most convicted offenders received a quick sentence to death by the gallows or to some form of corporal punishment such as branding, whipping, or the pillory. Prisons that were established in New York in 1819 and in Pennsylvania in 1829 offered an alternative to the death penalty and the cruelest of physical punishments for felons, while jails were used as place to sentence minor offenders. However, these alternatives still meant that the convicted offender had to receive and serve a sentence.

Tombstone gallows	*Early gallows*	*Pillory or stocks*	*Guillotine*

These traditional forms of punishment were a part of the common law heritage that Americans brought with them from England. However, that same heritage also included procedures, such as benefit of clergy, judicial reprieve, and recognizance, for mitigating the severity of punishments for those thought deserving of relief without being sentenced.

These procedures had never been formalized in England, but were used at the court's discretion, and their use increased over time. Thus, the concept of individualized justice by judicial prerogative had a basis in common law and, like many other common law practices, it was incorporated into American court procedures without being formalized by statute. Once prisons became established as a primary sentence for felons, the need to mitigate the harshness of that custodial environment offered additional support for judges to use probation as an alternative.

Recognizance

Recognizance was the procedure most frequently used by American judges. This required a convicted offender to enter into a bond agreement with the court (with or without posting security), pledging not to re-offend and to abide by other specific conditions for a specified period of time in return for release into the community. If the offender complied with his end of the agreement, the prescribed sentence was not imposed.

The first recorded practice of **recognizance** was by Judge Peter 0. Thatcher of the Municipal Court in Boston, Massachusetts in 1826. By the 1830s, Judge Thatcher was placing juvenile offenders under the supervision of the local sheriff or constable as a condition of release. By 1836, recognizance with sureties was included in the statutory law of Massachusetts as a discretionary alternative for sentencing judges, but with no specific requirement to guide its application.

Thus, the conceptual and applied aspects of probation were given form and direction. They developed within an authoritarian framework under the control of local judges, to be administered on a discretionary basis with individualized, rather than standardized expectations and resources. The early practices of **recognizance** were capricious, to say the least, but they did pave the way for the efforts which followed.

Probation Becomes Formalized

John Augustus, a successful Boston bootmaker, is credited in most of the literature as the Father of Probation because he established the practice more or less as it is used today. He was well respected in the community and well known about the courts, which he frequently visited to observe how justice was administered. Inspired by the temperance movement in Massachusetts, he began in the Boston Police Court in 1841 by having a convicted drunkard bailed to his custody for a specified period of time on the pledge that the man would remain sober. The man did remain sober and became a law abiding citizen. From this initial success, Augustus volunteered his services to the

Police Court and later the Municipal Court as a **probation officer,** until his death in 1859.

Augustus was the first to use the term **probation** as a period of trial release into the community in lieu of a sentence. He initiated the practice of casework for the court, which included presentence investigations to qualify candidates worthy of release, sentencing recommendations to the judge, supervision as an agent of the court, and efforts to reform the offender by developing rapport with him and providing him with guidance and direction (Augustus, 1852, 1939 reprint).

The practice of probation continued to grow and spread under the voluntary efforts of concerned individuals and agencies. In 1878, a Suffolk County statute mandated that the mayor of Boston appoint a probation officer from the police ranks to serve the court under the supervision of the police chief. Probation was available to any convicted offender "who may reasonably be expected to reform without punishment." No restrictions on eligibility were imposed. This law was extended in 1880 to give mayors of all cities and towns in Massachusetts the power to appoint a probation officer, but few did.

In 1891, the power to appoint Massachusetts probation officers was transferred from the mayors to the lower courts, with the stipulation that the officer be a member of the police force, but work directly under the supervision of the court. In 1898, the appointive power was vested in the Massachusetts superior courts.

These initial statutes authorized only the appointment of a probation officer and did not address a court's power to suspend sentence. That authority was assumed to exist in common law. In other states, the authority to suspend sentence was given to judges by statutes.

In 1897, the Missouri Legislature enacted a law allowing judges to suspend a sentence and grant probation at the county level. The Vermont Legislature enacted a similar law in 1898. Other states followed: Illinois, Minnesota, and Rhode Island in 1899; New Jersey in 1900, and New York in 1901. However, the Illinois and Minnesota laws provided only for juvenile probation to be administered by juvenile court judges at the county level. Vermont followed the county-administered plan, and provided for both juvenile and adult probation. Rhode Island established a unified state administered probation system and restricted probation eligibility to certain offenses. New York's original plan allowed all county courts to appoint probation officers.

It took until 1936 for this loosely structured method of providing probation services to be organized into a system of county probation departments, locally appointed and funded, but under the administration of the New York Department of Corrections.

By 1925, juvenile probation was authorized by statute in every state. However, in Wyoming, a separate juvenile court law and probation system was not authorized by statute until 1945. Legislation authorizing adult probation spread more slowly and did not exist nationwide until 1950. Nevertheless, probation was granted by some judges without the benefit of an authorizing statute. This same procedure was practiced in federal courts in at least sixty federal court districts in thirty-nine states.

A Legal Challenge to Probation

This practice of granting probation did not go unopposed, however. State and federal prosecutors contended that the judicial power to suspend sentence indefinitely had no basis in common law and, in fact, even statutes authorizing it were unconstitutional in that they infringed on the executive power to grant pardons.

The constitutionality of state legislatures having the power to authorize probation was upheld on appeal in New York in 1894. However, this did not settle the problem for other states nor the general question of judicial authority under common law. Finally, in 1916 the U.S. Supreme Court resolved that issue in the now famous **Killets case (*Ex Parte* United States, 242 U.S.27)**. By an unanimous decision authored by Chief Justice Edward D. White, the court held that federal courts **did not have the inherent power to suspend sentence** permanently or indefinitely and that there was no reason or right:

> … to continue a practice which is inconsistent with the Constitution since its exercise in the very nature of things amounts to a refusal by the judicial power to perform a duty resting upon it and, as a consequence thereof, to an interference with both the legislative and executive authority as fixed by the Constitution.

This decision meant that judges did not have the authority to suspend a sentence and/or grant probation unless that authority was given to them by the Legislature or Congress.

At the federal level, the debate continued over the legality of probation and the separation of powers for nine years. Finally, after thirty-four bills were introduced, the ***Federal Probation Act*** was passed in 1925. This established a uniform probation law at the federal level, but it was amended in 1930 to allow each federal district judge to appoint a probation officer as an agent of his court. The amendment also authorized these probation officers to undertake parole supervision and other related duties as requested by the United States Attorney General. This same structure remains today.

Disparity Spreads

Probation continued to develop within the various states at an uneven pace and with little uniformity in organization and staffing. As late as 1967, the President's Crime Commission reported that in thirty-two states juvenile probation was administered by local juvenile courts, in five states by state correctional agencies, in seven states by local welfare agencies, and by a mixture of state and local agencies in the remainder of the states.

Adult probation was state administered in combination with parole services in thirty states, administered by local courts in thirteen states, and by a mixture of state and local agencies in the remaining states (*Task Force Report: Corrections*, 1967, p. 35).

Probation Evolves in California

Outsiders frequently look to California as a leader in many fields of endeavor, as a prime mover. However, in the field of probation, California's development followed the course taken by other states summarized above.

Adult probation was first enacted in California in 1903, when criminal courts were authorized to **suspend the imposition of sentence** in cases of any person over the age of 16 if it appeared that there were circumstances in mitigation, or that "the ends of justice will be subserved thereby." No other eligibility qualifications were placed on those granted probation.

Thus, as in other states, the grant of probation was given to the court by the Legislature, but judges had discretion as to the length of its duration, and for adults this could extend up to the maximum prison term provided for the crime. Each local judge was authorized to appoint any officer of a charitable organization or any citizen to serve as his probation officer without compensation. Such officers had the power of arrest without a warrant *"if the interests of justice so requires, and if the court in its judgment, shall have reason to believe that conditions are violated or that the defendant is engaging in criminal practices, or has become abandoned to improper associates or a vicious life"* (*California Statute*, 1903, p. 685).

In that same year, 1903, California's first juvenile court law was enacted and placed, almost as an afterthought, in the appendix of the Penal Code. Thus, both adult and juvenile probation were created, in theory at least. However, as a compromise to resistance against probation in the Legislature, authors of the probation bills agreed to an amendment "whereby public funds could not be used to pay probation officers" (Lemert, 1970, p. 38).

The role of a probation officer was cast in an authoritarian setting under the control of local courts. No special qualifications were required of those who served in this role. Who was selected, how probation was administered, and even whether or not probation existed was a concern initially left to local courts.

As it is with many features of the justice system, the present organization and administration of probation is the result of an historical accident. Placing it under the control of local courts, of fifty-eight fiefdoms, erected an almost insurmountable barrier to achieving uniformity in its application.

State Efforts to Control Adult Probation

Concern was aroused by 1923 that adult probation was not being used by local courts as intended. A lack of uniformity in adult probation practices was left to local remedies, while legislation was increasingly aimed at limiting the sentencing authority of local judges.

Prior to 1923, there were no restrictions on the eligibility of offenders for probation and local judges had complete discretion to suspend sentence. A 1923 statute limited eligibility and denied judge the authority to grant probation to persons in cases of: murder, robbery, burglary, or rape, "....wherein the perpetration of such crimes a deadly weapon was used or where the perpetrator was armed with a deadly weapon . . . to any person previously convicted of any of the above crimes .. . to any public official who offered or took a bribe."

In 1927, judges were denied authority to grant probation to any offender with a prior felony conviction or to any person possessing a weapon during the commission of a crime or when arrested. As a person familiar with the cheeky nature of judges and their penchant for exceeding judicial authority, it was not surprising to read that they found various methods to sidestep the statutory restrictions on their power to suspend sentence.

These circumventions were seriously addressed by the California Crime Commission appointed by the Legislature in 1929. The commission noted the widespread disparity in sentencing practices between counties and judges.

The Post War Years

Probation and court procedures received little attention during the war years. However, by 1948 state officials again turned their attention to how corrections was administered in California. Two Special Crime Study Commissions were appointed: one on adult services and one on juvenile justice. They in turn appointed a Committee for the Study of Probation Services in California. The Committee found a tremendous range of differences among county probation departments in terms of organization, staff, funding, and responsibilities. (*Probation Services in California*, 1949).

In short, standards did not exist and the quality of probation work was questionable. Nevertheless, the Committee encouraged an increase in the use of probation, particularly at the municipal and juvenile court levels as a far more economical alternative than institutional commitments. The annual per capita cost for an adult in prison was $1,000, and for juveniles in the California Youth Authority (CYA) it was $2,000, compared to $96 a year for probation supervision. However, no specific recommendations were made beyond taking steps to "remedy the deficiencies summarized" (*Probation Services in California*, 1949, p. 43).

The Probation Subsidy

In late 1961, a legislative committee on criminal procedures approached the State Board of Corrections and requested assistance in developing a program that would improve correctional services at the county level and yet would be cost-effective for the state (Smith, 1971, p. 24). After some preliminary study and debate, the Legislature directed the Board of Corrections, in 1963, to conduct a statewide study of probation and identify the critical problems and their solutions (Smith, 1971, p. 4). The problems identified by the board were excessive caseloads, inadequate supervision of staff, inadequate secretarial services, lack of an offender classification system, and limited resources to support intensive supervision efforts.

At the conclusion of its study in 1964, the Board made four recommendations that were regarded as critical if needed changes were to occur (*Probation Study*, 1964, p. 12).

> ➤ special probation supervision
> ➤ training and certification of personnel
> ➤ county regional correctional institutions
> ➤ delinquency and crime prevention programs.

The recommendation of *special probation supervision* became the essence of the **1965 Probation Subsidy Law** by which participating counties were paid between $2,800 and $4,000 for each offender, adult or juvenile, not committed to state institutions who otherwise might have been committed, and who instead were supervised on probation.

This subsidy approach was accepted by the Legislature and Governor as a cost effective means to limit taxes, while at the same time providing more effective probation supervision. The $4,000 paid to counties certainly was less than the $8,000 - $12,000 needed to keep each offender in an institution for a year. Also, institutional populations were reaching their limit. Consequently, expensive capital outlay would not be required if populations were to be reduced. Under the budget trimming efforts of Governor Ronald Reagan, the subsidy program flourished.

The three remaining recommendations were ignored in the 1965 law, which suggests that the Legislature's primary concern was economy for the state, not equity in probation services. However, the law did mandate that the California Youth Authority (CYA) adopt and implement minimum standards for the operation of special probation supervision units (Smith, 1971, p. 36).

The standards imposed limited caseload sizes to fifty offenders per officer and six officers per supervisor, and required the use of some formal classification and treatment method to match offender needs with supervision resources. Generous clerical and support staff was also provided (Smith, 1971, pp. 36-64; Lemert & Dill, 1978, p. 99).

In addition to the prescribed standards, officers were encouraged to use innovative supervision techniques and treatment approaches. In support of these mandates, CYA provided training to local officers selected for special supervision in a variety of classification and treatment models.

Selection of officers to staff the special units usually was on the basis of seniority, and usually it meant a promotion to the position of PO III, and a pay increase. Usually, but not always, even this required standardization was not uniformly implemented by local agencies.

The initial impact of the subsidy program was a significant reduction in state institutional commitments, as intended. By 1970, however, the selection of personnel to staff special supervision shifted away from seniority and experience, and less critical screening was used in selecting the type of offenders who qualified for special supervision. The entire "special" process became routinized and the program became a method of serving other organizational needs, such as "training, enhancement of morale, reduction of internal tensions (and) workload equalization" (Lemert & Dill, 1978, p. 133).

It is beyond the scope of this chapter to present the subsidy program in more detail or to evaluate its results. Suffice it to say that the probation subsidy programs were gradually phased out for many reasons. The more that offenders were diverted into a subsidy program, the more the probation violation rate increased. As violations increased and probationers were then sentenced to jail or prison, subsidy funds decreased. It had a spiraling effect. (Peoples, 1982).

That the subsidy program achieved some worthwhile goals cannot be denied. The taxpayers saved some money during the years of its operation. Many offenders received more humane dispositions by not going to prison or juvenile institutions. Also, many probation officers received an array of training and came to perceive their role in more professional terms. However, standardization did not replace disparity, and professionalism remained a term that probation officers assumed, but did not completely achieve.

The few standards that were mandated were still implemented under the theme of local control. Caseload sizes continued to vary. The array of classification and treatment methods used were often unrelated to the needs of the client or were used only in token compliance to the program (Lemert & Dill, 1978, pp. 135-145).

By the mid-1970s, the mood of the Governor, the Legislature, and the public, had moved toward a more punitive approach in response to an increasing crime and delinquency rate and an increasing rate of probation violations by those under supervision in subsidy programs. Special supervision of offenders, both juvenile and adult, withered on the vine. By 1977, rehabilitation as a goal was replaced by punishment in the passage of the **Determinate Sentence Law**, which also placed substantial limits of who could receive a grant of probation. Additional limits have been added in subsequent legislation.

Summary

As we have seen, probation developed over many years from a haphazard approach used by judicial discretion to its current status wherein every state offers both juvenile and adult probation services, some operating at the state level and some at the county level. In California, each county has a probation department, with a juvenile division and an adult division (except in San Francisco, where separate departments exist for adult and juvenile services). Many of the procedures of probation have been standardized, particularly in the areas of presentence investigations and reports, and in juvenile procedures. The subsidy program sounded good on its face, but it was motivated more by economic concerns than by concerns to achieve a viable probation system.

The current structures and procedures of probation in California and the roles and responsibilities of probation officers are the subjects of Chapters 2 and 3.

References

Andrews, William. *Old Time Punishments*. London: William C. Andrews & Co., 1890. Reprinted and distributed by Crown Publishers of New York.

Augustus, John. *A Report of the Labors of John Augustus for the Last Ten Years in Aid of the Unfortunate*. Boston: Wright & Hasty, 1852. Reprinted as *John Augustus, First Probation Officer*. New York: National Probation Association, 1939.

Dressler, David. *Practice and Theory of Probation and Parole.* 2ⁿᵈ ed. New York: Columbia University Press, 1969.

Hibbert, Christopher. *The Roots of Evil: A Social History of Crime and Punishment.* Boston: Little, Brown , 1957.

Killinger, George C. & Paul F. Cromwell, Jr. *Penology: The Evolution of Corrections in America.* St. Paul: West Publishing, 1973.

Lemert, Edwin M. *Social Action and Legal Change: Revolution within the Juvenile Court.* Chicago: Aldine Publishing, 1970.

Lemert, Edwin M., and Forrest Dill. *Offenders in the Community: The Probation Subsidy in California.* Lexington, MA: D. C. Heath, 1978.

McGee, Richard & Robert Montilla. *Organization of State Correctional Services in the Control and Treatment of Crime and Delinquency.* Sacramento: Youth & Adult Corrections Agency, 1967.

Peoples, Edward E. *The Development of California's Standards and Training for Corrections Program: A Case Study in Institution Building.* Doctoral dissertation, University of Southern California, 1982.

The Practioner in Corrections. Sacramento, CA: California Probation, Parole and Correctional Association, 1964

California Board of Corrections Publications

Burdman, Milton; Winslow Rouse and Stuart Adams. *Probation in California.* Sacramento: California Board of Corrections, 1957.

The Board of Corrections Probation Study of 1964, Final Report. Sacramento: State Printing Office, 1971

The California Correctional System Study, Final Report. Sacramento: State Printing Office, 1971.

Coordinated California Corrections: Field Services Task Force Report. Sacramento: State Printing Office, 1971

Government Reports

President's Commission on Law Enforcement and Administration of Justice. *Task Force Report: Corrections.* Washington, D. C.: Government Printing Office, 1967

Special Crime Study Commission. *Probation Services in California, 1948.* Sacramento: State Printing Office, 1949.

Special Study Commission on Correctional Facilities and Services*: Probation in California.* Sacramento: State Printing Office, 1957

Internet References

http://probation.co.la.ca.us/anmviewer.asp?a=4&z=3
Presents an interesting summary of the history of Los Angeles County probation

http://www.calebi.com/probation.htm
Offers selected probation department web sites

http://probation.countyofventura.org/History.htm
Presents a history of Ventura County probation

http://www.appa-net.org/category3.html
Offers an array of web sites showing the various locations of probation agencies in the U. S.

http://www.henrycty.com/codepartments/courtservices/history.html
Gives a brief history of probation

http://www.cya.ca.gov/DivisionsBoards/DJJ/about/history/histindex.htm
Presents a slide show of CYA's history

Case Decision

Ex Parte (Killets) v. United States, 242 U.S.27 (1916)

Chapter 2: Adult Probation Investigation Services

Key Terms and Concepts

Aggravated term	Home supervision	Probation conditions
Cite-and-release	Indeterminate sentence	Punishment
Determinate sentence	Instant offense	Recidivist
Discretionary release	Mitigated term	Rehabilitation
Disparity	OR	Sentencing
Drug diversion	Presentence report	Shock probation
Expungement	Probation	Supervised OR

Introduction

This chapter will focus on the structure, roles, and responsibilities of adult probation and the investigation services in California. Probation services can be divided into two primary functions: **investigation** and **supervision**. At the adult level, probation officers become involved in certain pretrial procedures, and then become extensively involved in presentence procedures, as the investigative arm of the court. They continue their involvement during probation supervision, as the enforcement/treatment arm of the court.

At the juvenile level, they become involved almost immediately after an arrest, and their involvement continues throughout the entire court process, and beyond, to include supervision and/or placement. However, both adult and juvenile probation officers apply the current adult sentencing terms and procedures while performing their investigative functions. Consequently, the discussion of sentencing laws and their application in this chapter applies equally to juvenile proceedings, with some slight variations in terminology.

This chapter examines judicial sentencing and the alternative procedures, including the types of sentencing laws and sentencing options in both misdemeanor and felony cases. Pre-trial services that probation performs for the court are covered as well, and include cite-and-release programs, OR investigations, and home supervision, pending trial.

Sentencing

Sentencing is one of the most important functions of the justice system, because it affects not only the life of the offender, but the feelings of the victim, and the safety of the community. The goals of sentencing are many. However, two primary goals are reflected in California's sentencing practices: rehabilitation and punishment.

Types of Sentencing Laws

There are two basic types of felony sentencing laws used in California.

> ➤ Indeterminate sentence
> ➤ Determinate sentence

Each type of sentencing law is related to a particular goal that the Legislature had in mind when it was enacted.

The Indeterminate Sentence Law

Historically, the indeterminate sentence law has always been associated with parole and the goal of **rehabilitation**. California enacted the **Indeterminate Sentence Law (ISL)** in 1917, when it initiated parole, and considered parole as an extension of the offender's sentence into the community after serving some portion of it in prison.

The ISL is a sentencing law in which the Legislature sets a minimum and a maximum for the offender to serve, and a parole board conducts an annual review of the inmate's progress toward rehabilitation to determine when the optimum time is for his or her release. The Parole Board has the discretionary authority to grantconditional release. The Governor, however, may over-ride the Board's decision.

For example, a sentence might be from five years to life or one to ten years. Somewhere within those limits, the offender knew he or she could get parole when rehabilitated. If an offender was kept too long, he or she might become bitter and angry. If released too soon, he or she might not yet be rehabilitated. The use of this law created a great deal of disparity and did not prove effective in the rehabilitative process. The **recidivist rate** (rate of return to prison) was approximately seventy percent.

There were many individuals and groups criticizing the ISL and attempting to enact a replacement law. At one time during the 1970s, individuals representing a wide spectrum of interests met to write a new law. They included Ed Davis, then Chief of Police for Los Angeles, a conservative law-and-order person, Jan Morrison, a member of the American Friends Society (Quakers), a humanist organization, and members of the Prisoner's Union in San Francisco, all calling for the abolition of the ISL.

The conservatives wanted longer prison terms and the Quakers wanted fair and equal punishment. By 1977, their influence combined with the punitive feelings of the Governor, the Legislature, and the public, prompted legislation that changed how convicted felons were sentenced. Legislation was enacted that limited the use of the ISL and established the Determinate Sentence Law as the primary method of sentencing convicted felons.

The Determinate Sentence Law

On July 1, 1977, the ISL became limited in application, and the **Determinate Sentence Law (DSL)** took effect. Its goals are spelled out clearly in the following portion of Penal Code §1170:

> The Legislature finds and declares that the purpose of imprisonment for crime is **punishment**. This purpose is best served by terms proportionate to the seriousness of the offense with provision for uniformity in the sentences of offenders committing the same offense under similar circumstances. The Legislature further finds and declares that the **elimination of disparity** and the provision of uniformity of sentences can best be achieved by determinate sentences fixed by statute in proportion to the seriousness of the offense.

Let **the punishment fit the crime**. The DSL is a type of sentencing law in which the Legislature determined **three specific prison terms** for each felony: a minimum term (**mitigating**), a medium term (**presumptive**), and a maximum term (**aggravated**). The judge was to choose the middle term unless he or she could find factors in either mitigation or aggravation. Release on parole was mandatory when the inmate had served his or her time, less any good time or work time credits.

In choosing either the minimum or maximum term, the sentencing judge would assess the case based on a list of either mitigating or aggravating factors from a list prepared by the state's Judicial Council. Between its inception in 1977 and January 22, 2007, the specific prison term given a defendant was based on a judge's evaluation of the appropriate factors, as summarized to the judge by the investigating deputy probation officer. However, none of these factors needed to be considered at trial in determining the conviction.

On January 22, 2007, the U. S. Supreme Court overturned the portion of California's DSL that allowed judges to consider aggravating factors from the usual list unless those factors were proven to a jury at trial. The case on appeal was a California case in which a former Richmond, California police officer was convicted of continuous sexual abuse of a child under the age of 14 years. The prescribed DSL prison terms were either 6, 12, or 16 years. The judge reviewed the factors and chose the 16-year sentence. On appeal, the U. S. Supreme Court held that:

> The DSL, by placing sentence-elevating fact-finding within the judge's province, violates a defendant's right to trial by jury safeguarded by the Sixth and Fourteenth Amendments (*Cunningham v. California*, 2007).

The decision applies **retroactively** to all sentenced felons, which means that approximately 10,000 prison inmates will either be paroled early, using the middle prison time as a guide, or will receive new jury trials around the aggravating factors. Ironically, the Governor who led the efforts to establish the DSL, making punishment fit the crime, Jerry Brown, is now the state's Attorney General, and must lead the way in deciding how to proceed with releasing or re-trying the currently imprisoned inmates.

In a similar ruling on January 23, 2007, California's Sixth Appellate Court held that a prior juvenile record may not be used as an aggravating factor (as before) for purposes of adult sentencing unless that juvenile record was obtained by the juvenile's admission at court, or by a jury of six or more of one's peers. (***People v. Nguyen,*** **2007**).

As of this writing, legislation (SB40) has been introduced to modify the DSL to remove the requirement that judges must choose the middle term unless mitigating or aggravating factors are considered, and gives judges complete discretion to choose any sentence within a range of times set by law. This change will streamline sentencing, but it still does not require judges to base their sentences on facts presented to a jury, a key part of the Supreme Court's ruling. Consequently, the new sentencing law will be open to legal challenges and additional legislation might be required.

There are still several indeterminate sentence crimes, including, but not limited to murder, kidnap for ransom, the two-strike and three-strike crimes, and certain sex crimes per §667.61 PC. A defendant who receives one of these ISL terms usually must serve two-thirds of the minimum time before being eligible for parole, and parole in these cases is at the discretion of the Parole Board. It is called **discretionary release**.

Under the DSL, all the offender needs to do is to serve the time given by the judge and release is automatic and cannot be denied, regardless of the inmate's attitude or intentions. In addition, there is a work-time law that allows an inmate to earn up to one day off for each day worked, and everyone is given the opportunity to work. Participation in educational or vocational programs is equated with working for purposes of earning half-time off of a sentence. However, in certain violent crimes, the defendant must serve up to eighty-five percent of the sentenced time before being eligible for parole.

The DSL also placed certain limits on who is eligible to receive probation. One Penal Code section mandates prison as the sentence for a violation of certain listed violent offenses (§1203.06 PC) that include the personal use of a firearm. This is known as the *use-a-gun-go-to-prison-law*, and judges do not have discretion in sentencing. Probation is not an option.

As was mentioned in Chapter 1, judges prefer not to have legislative restraints interfere with their discretionary authority. In 1977, Judge Reagan, then a superior court judge in San Mateo County, had before him for sentencing a young defendant who used a gun in the commission of a bank robbery. In the judge's mind, there were many extenuating circumstances, and the judge believed that the defendant was a good candidate for probation. The prosecutor pointed out the mandatory wording in the law, but the judge indicated that the Legislature did not really mean to strip judges of their discretion in sentencing offenders.

The judge suspended the sentence and granted the defendant probation for a period of five years. The prosecutor appealed (***People v. Tanner, 1979***), and the California Supreme Court agreed with the prosecutor and reversed the judge's action. This case reaffirmed the **1916** *Killets* case precedent, discussed in Chapter 1, that many judges had overlooked; namely, that judges are able to grant probation only in cases where the Legislature enacts statues giving them the authority to suspend a sentence (***U.S., ExParte, 1916***). Fortunately the probationer Tanner was allowed to complete probation. He did well and did not re-offend.

California's Public Safety Realignment Plan

It is appropriate at this point in your reading to provide a summary of A.B 109, signed into law by Governor Brown and effective October 1, 2011. As stated in the *Preface*, this statute and it's trailers make **the most significant changes in criminal procedures in thirty-five** years. It will affect felony sentencing, county jail populations and jail credits, probation sentencing recommendations, and post-release supervision and parole.

The summary is provided below and we will refer to it in the discussions of relevant contents in subsequent chapters. For a comprehensive discussion of this legislation, see Garrick Byers' article *Realignment*, cited at the end of this chapter and from which this summary is taken.

The main sentencing provisions are:

- The term felony has been redefined to mean an offense punishable by death or by imprisonment in the state prison or by imprisonment in the county jail for more than a year. PC §17.

- Sentences for most felonies that are non-serious, non-violent and non-registerable sex offenses (**so-called non-non-non felonies**), if the defendant also has no prior serious, violent or registerable convictions, will now be served in the county jail. See PC §1170(h)(2)-(3). (The length of felony terms have not changed.)

- Felonies with non-specified terms in the underlying statute will be punishable by a term of 16 months, 2 years or 3 years in the county jail. PC §§18; 1170(h)(1). Sentences for these offenses may include a period of county jail and a period of probation not to exceed the maximum possible term. PC §1170(h)(5).

- Probation deferred entry of judgment and other alternatives to prison continue to be available sentencing options.

- County jail terms of more than 1 year for a felony are priorable as a sentencing enhancement. PC §667.5(b).

- All county jail inmates except convicted murderers and those being committed to state prison for violent felonies can earn 50 percent conduct credits under PC §4019.

- Counties may permit electronic monitoring in lieu of bail (PC §1203.018) or home detention in lieu of jail (PC §1203.016). Time on electronic monitoring or home detention counts toward mandatory minimum sentences. PC §2900.5.

- There are 59 felony offenses that are non-serious, nonviolent and non-registerable sex offenses that are nonetheless punishable by a term in prison. These offenses generally involve a weapon or injury.

- Individuals convicted of a current or prior serious or violent offense, required to register under PC §290 or whose sentence is enhanced under PC §186.11 (taking more than $100,000 under certain circumstances) must serve their current term in prison. PC §1170(h)(3).

- Individuals sentenced to consecutive terms where one term (whether principal or subordinate) is punishable by state prison must serve the aggregate sentence in prison. PC §1170.1(a). (No statutory provision yet addresses concurrent sentences.)

The main post-release and parole provisions operative October 1, 2011 are:

- Individuals convicted of felonies punishable by a prescribed term of county jail in the underlying statute will not be supervised after release; there will be no period of parole.

- Only those individuals convicted of a straight felony (where the term is not prescribed by the underlying statute and, therefore, is 16 months, 2 years or 3 years under PC §1170(h)(1)) may be sentenced to a period of county jail and a period of probation not to exceed the maximum

  possible term. PC §1170(h)(5). See Legislative Counsel's Digest to A.B.

116 (Cal Stats 2011, ch 136).

- Prison sentences for non-non-non felonies will be followed by a period of up to 3 years of Post-release Community Supervision administered by the counties. Violations of Post Release Community Supervision can be punished in many ways, including flash incarceration. Revocations must be done by a new Court Revocation Officer. PC §§3450-3458.

- Offenders released from state prison after serving a sentence for a third strike or a serious or violent felony or who are classified as high risk sex offenders or mentally disordered or who are on parole prior to October 1, 2011 will be under state parole supervision. See PC §§3000.08, 3000.09.

- Parole revocations will be served in county jail for a maximum of 180 days.

- Only persons previously sentenced to a term of life can be returned to prison on a parole revocation.

Beginning July 1, 2013, the parole revocation process will become a county court-based process. Until then, parole revocations will continue under the Board of Parole Hearings.

After July 1, 2013, the BPH will be responsible for:

- Parole considerations for lifers

- Medical parole hearings

- Mentally disordered offender cases; and

- Sexually violent predator cases

The Division of Juvenile Justice is unaffected by realignment. See Legislative Counsel's Digest for A.B. 117 (Cal Stats 2011, ch. 39).

The Sentencing Process

After a felony conviction, either by verdict or plea, the matter is set for a sentencing hearing. During the time between the verdict and sentencing, the case is referred by the court to the probation department for an investigation and report of the probation officer (**RPO**), as to the proper sentence.

The Presentence Report

The probation officer (PO) and his or her deputies serve as the investigative arms of the court during the **presentence process**. When a convicted offender has been referred for the sentencing investigation, the case is assigned to a deputy probation officer, who works in the **Investigation Unit**, to complete the RPO.

The probation officer will conduct a thorough investigation into the nature of the crime, the role of the defendant and codefendants, if any, and the social and personal life of the defendant. All the significant information collected by the probation officer is summarized in what is called a **presentence report**.

The report contains the details about the offense, the defendant's statement as to his or her role in it and motives for it, victim impact statement, an assessment of a prior record, if any, and the potential of the defendant to reform. The PO must also evaluate the various mitigating and aggravating factors if a prison term is likely under the DSL. However, the exact role of the PO in this process is yet to be worked out in light of the U. S. Supreme Court's recent *Cunningham* ruling about the DSL.

The RPO is one of the most important documents filed with the court. Since the judge knows nothing about those ninety percent (plus) of the cases in which the defendants are convicted by plea bargain, he or she must rely on the RPO to provide all the relevant information upon which to base a sentence. The information also will be used later, either in developing a plan for probation supervision, or for prison classification. It will also be considered later in determining

Sample Presentence Report

Hearing Date: January 31, 2007

In the Superior Court of the State of California
In and for the County of Lilliput

The People of the State of California)   Probation File # 007
                         Plaintiff)   Court # 13244

                    vs.   Probation Officer's
                                              Presentence Report

John Henry Doe
                    Defendant)

_____

Present Offense: Violation of Penal Code Section 484-487, grand theft.

Complaint: A felony complaint was filed in court on December 13, 2006, charging the present offense.

Defense Attorney: Peter Slickhammer

Court Process: The defendant was arraigned on December 15, and the case was continued to December 20 for plea and to set. On that date, he waived his right to a preliminary hearing, he was then held to answer, and the matter was set for further proceedings on December 24.

Plea: The defendant entered a plea of guilty on December 24.

Arrest and Custody Status: The defendant was arrested on December 11, 2006 for grand theft by, Samuel Spade, Jr., security officer at Jenny's Store and was booked in county jail by Lilliput police officers. He was released later that day by the probation department's cite-and-release officer.

Circumstances of Offense:
        Reports and investigation by the probation officer show that in the late afternoon of December 11, the defendant was under surveillance by the security officer at the place of his employment, Jenny's Store. Near the end of his shift, he was observed to remove some cash from the register and place it in his pocket. He then walked toward the exit door, at the end of his shift, and was stopped and arrested by security. He denied taking any money. He

2

was escorted to the store's office by security, where he was asked to empty his pockets. He placed $450. on the desk, began crying, and admitted taking the money. He also admitted intending to take up to $1,500. more during the week.

The defendant had been under surveillance by store security as a suspect in thefts from his register over the past two months. A total of $1,200. was missing during that time.

Defendant's Statement:

The defendant freely admitted stealing all the money in question over a two month period. He had hoped that business would be better so as to make the thefts less obvious, but was in a real need of the money to make the current and back payments on his car to avoid having it repossessed. In the past he had always relied on his mother for money to support his lifestyle, but on this occasion he wanted to make it on his own. He considers that he committed the thefts in a moment of weakness and has learned his lesson. He agreed to comply with any and all conditions of probation that the court might impose, and requested that he be granted probation.

Prior Record:

The defendant was arrested by Lilliput sheriff's deputies on October 13, 2006, pursuant to a warrant charging petty theft. On this occasion, he was observed taking a $700. Gateway computer from Jenny's Store, where he worked. He delivered it to a customer and was paid cash by the customer. He failed to record the sales transaction and kept the cash. Store security indicates that this was the third instance in which the defendant took merchandise from the store and delivered it to customers, receiving cash in return, for a total loss to the store of $1,650. A complaint was filed in Lilliput County Court in these matters, but the complaint was dismissed in the interests of justice in light of his guilty plea to the instant offense.

The defendant currently is under investigation by CHP as a suspect in arson and fraud charges resulting from an incident on August 13, 2006, in which a 2005 BMW, registered to the defendant, was totally destroyed by fire. The defendant was behind four months on the car payments, but insurance covered the loss.

This officer made a personal visit to the Maligña Police Department in the small town where the defendant was raised. He had no juvenile record, and was never considered a behavior problem in the community.

3

Residence: The defendant relates that for the past two years he has rented from, and lived in the rear house on property owned by his sister and her husband in Lilliput township. Prior to that, he lived with his mother in Maligña

Family Background: The following information comes from interviews with the defendant and his mother. He is the second of two children of Harvey and Mildred Zeta-Doe from Maligña. His parents divorced when he was fourteen, after his father ran off with the mother's best friend. The mother received a substantial divorce settlement from her husband and has since lived very well. Since then, the mother has been a controlling and domineering influence in the defendant's life, making most all his decisions, yet at the same time providing him with all the luxuries money could buy.

The defendant's mother relates that she admittedly resented being abandoned by her husband and has since done what she could to hold on to her son . She realizes that she must let him go and allow him to grow up. She will cooperate with probation in any way to help him succeed if probation is granted.

Education: It has been verified that the defendant graduated from Maligña High School in 2001. He maintained a 3.0 grade point average, although he did not take a college prep tract and took as many shop classes as he could. Also his grades dropped from As to Bs and even Cs in his senior year. The vice principal, Horace Manné, related that the defendant was never considered a behavior problem.

The defendant relates that he attended Lilliput Community College full time for two semesters right out of high school, but did not do well and dropped out of school. He states that he might return to college if and when he can find some direction in life.

Marital Status: Single, always.

Military Service: The defendant relates that he served nearly two years in the Army National Guard, but was discharged for medical reasons in June 2005. Army National Guard records show that he received a less than honorable discharge in June 2005 after he was caught stealing from the guard's commissary while at his annual two-week training camp, and just prior to his unit being shipped out to Iraq. The sergeant in his local guard relates that the unofficial version suggests the belief that he stole in a way that assured him getting caught so that he could avoid going to Iraq.

4

Though charges were dropped, he also took money from his employer by delivering merchandise to several customers, and pocketing the cash. He also is a suspect in the arson and fraud case in which his BMW was destroyed by fire. It appears that these thefts were the result of his need to maintain a high lifestyle on a basic store salary, while at the same time trying to become independent of his mother's support.

Probation is recommended for several reasons. He has no prior official record and it seems that his criminal bent is of recent expression. He has no juvenile record. He expresses complete cooperation with the court and probation, and shows some semblance of guilt and contrition. The causes of his dysfunctional behavior might run deep, and probation supervision should be intensive. He undoubtedly will require some type of counseling to help him develop independence and self-direction, and the maturity to live within his financial means.

Restitution is an issue in this case in that the defendant admits to taking $1,650. of the store's money in exchange for merchandise that was delivered but for which no sales record was made. He denies taking the $1,200. on any earlier date.

The defendant's attorney indicates that at the time of sentencing, he will make a motion to the court to declare this offense to be a misdemeanor, thereby avoiding a felony conviction that could hurt his future opportunities in life. This officer appreciates the negative effect that a felony conviction might have, but reminds the court that the offense can always be reduced to a misdemeanor if and when the defendant completes probation, That record can then be expunged.

Recommendations:

The Probation Officer respectfully recommends that:

The imposition of judgment be suspended for a period of three years, and

The defendant be granted formal probation subject to the standard conditions and the following special conditions:

That he submit his person, place of residence, and automobile to search at any time for any enforcement purpose by any peace officer, without a warrant;

Parole conditions, and perhaps much later in preparing any subsequent presentence reports, if the defendant re-offends.

The law requires a RPO in felony cases, and makes it discretionary in misdemeanor cases. However, most probation departments are too busy and overworked with felony matters to have the time to deal with misdemeanor investigations. Often these reports consist of a one-page fill-in, with sentencing recommendations.

If the probation officer recommends probation, he or she will include a list of the terms and conditions that he or she thinks should be made a part of the probation order. If the defendant is not eligible for probation, the probation officer will recommend whatever sentence is legally required. Now, **pursuant to AB 109**, felony offenders convicted of any of the so-called **non-non-non offenses** may be sentenced to jail, jail plus probation, or home detention. Electronic monitoring will undoubtedly come into play more often than before because of the potential for increased jail populations and probation case loads.

The above sample presentence report reflects a basic case in which the defendant was cooperative, the investigation was quick and easy, and the recommendation was typical. Even so, note what pieces of information were verified and what were hearsay. Also note what subtle bits of information might influence a judge in sentencing. As a reader, imagine yourself as a probation officer completing about 20 of these investigations and reports each month, with many being more completed that this one above.

The Sentencing Hearing

The probation officer's report is filed with the court, and the judge must sign it, stating that he or she has read and considered the report. Copies also are given to the prosecution and the defense so that they can prepare any arguments about sentencing at the sentencing hearing. At the hearing, either side may present additional evidence that they want the judge to consider, and they may argue for or against the recommendation of the probation officer. The judge then proceeds to either pronounce sentence or grant probation.

Sentencing Options

The law is very clear about what sentences crimes may receive. Misdemeanors are punishable by a jail term of up to one year, or by fine, or by both jail and fine. However, in reality, most misdemeanants receive probation and/or electronic monitoring, or a fine. Felonies are punishable by one of the prison times provided by the determinate sentence law, and the **non-non-non felonies** are punishable by a term in county jail. However, many convicted felons receive probation or jail plus probation as a sentence.

There are a number of crimes that are categorized as being non-violent, non-serious, and non-sex offenses but nonetheless, under the California Penal Code, will still require that offenders serve their sentences in State prisons. These crimes are also known as the **Exclusions**, and there are a total of 59. Their exclusion status is due to their enactment as majority-vote bills wherein voters decided that tougher and longer sentences were required for certain kinds of offenses. Thus, any offender convicted of any one of these 59 exclusions will serve their sentences with the State, and they will be released under parole supervision.

Adults under the age of 21 years from criminal court, and juveniles from juvenile court may also be referred for this type of study to the Division of Juvenile Facilities. The report from either facility will provide a diagnostic evaluation of the defendant, and a recommendation about the appropriate disposition.

Probation Services for Adults

One might think that by its very name and/or definition, probation comes into play after conviction. It usually does. However, there are three situations in which adult probation officers serve the court even before any trial or related proceedings. These are the cite-and-release, bail, and OR investigations, which are discussed below.

Cite-and-Release, Bail, and OR Investigations

When individuals are arrested by police and booked into jail, the first thing they want to do is get out. Some post bail, and others use the bail bond system. Also, many jurisdictions operate some form of a **cite-and-release program** on a 24-hour basis in order to reduce the jail

Let me out!! I'm innocent, I tell you, I'm innocent!!

population as much as possible. In many counties this program is staffed by probation officers. They will interview the prisoner after booking to determine whether further detention is needed. They consider the likelihood of the person appearing in court when required. In doing this, they look for stability and ties in the area such as family, property, and employment.

They also look at the person's prior record to determine if they have ever failed to appear (have any **FTAs** in the record) on previous release occasions. They also consider the risk to public safety that the person might pose if released. This would include whether they were armed during the commission of the **instant offense** (offense for which they were arrested), the severity of the instant offense, whether they were on probation or parole at the time, and the concerns of any victim, particularly in domestic violence cases.

The cite-and-release staff usually has criteria to use in assessing the worthiness of the person for release, as well as limits on their release authority. If the person qualifies for release, he or she is given a citation to appear in court, similar to what the arresting officer could have given. A court appearance date is provided on the citation. After signing it, the person is released without bond or bail.

Some arrested persons do not qualify for cite-and-release and must remain in jail until they either post bail or are released by the judge after their initial court appearance and arraignment. Immediately after arraignment in court, the defense attorney will make a motion to have his or her client's bail lowered, or to have the client released on what is termed **own recognizance (OR)**. That is a release of the person on his or her written promise to return to court when required. Usually, the judge knows nothing about the defendant at this point, and wants additional information about him or her in order to rule appropriately on the motion.

The proceedings will be continued for a day or two, and the matter will be referred to the county probation officer, who serves as the investigative arm of the court, for an **OR investigation** and report. Some jurisdictions have created independent investigative units, working out of the court, to complete the OR investigations. In most cases, a deputy probation officer, working in the investigation unit, will investigate the defendant's background and make a recommendation to the court about how to rule on the defense's motion, based on the defendant's ties in the area, potential for harm to the victim or others, and the likelihood that he or she will return to court when required.

Based on the investigating officer's recommendation, the judge may grant the motion for OR release, deny the motion, but lower the bail, raise the bail, or order that the defendant be denied bail.

In recent years, the county jail populations in most counties have increased to the point where there just is no bed space left. Many counties simply cannot afford to build a new jail, given today's high construction costs. The populations inside the jails, that once represented the full range of offenders, from the hard core to the lightweight, are now primarily the serious and violent offenders. Minor offenders are either cited by the police or the jail's cite-and-release staff.

In fact, in many cases some of the less violent serious offenders must be cited out to make room for those more violent. Consequently, there is a category of defendants, whose number is increasing, who cannot be fully trusted in the community, but whose behavior is not serious or threatening enough to warrant complete detention.

In response to this, many jurisdictions have established a creative method of releasing these defendants from jail, pending trial, called **Supervised OR**. These offenders are released without having to post bond, but they must agree to abide by certain **conditions and supervision** by the enforcement arm of the court, the probation officer, until their case has been settled. Conditions might include anti-narcotic/drug testing, non-association with certain other individuals, a restriction from certain locations, electronic monitoring, curfew, a requirement to submit to search at any time, and any other condition that the judge or probation officer thinks is appropriate.

A violation of any condition could result in the judge revoking the supervised OR status and ordering jail confinement.

This supervised OR continues until the case is settled by trial or other means, which often takes months or up to a year or more. It is far cheaper to have one probation officer supervise 75 to 100 OR defendants than it is to keep them housed in a jail. Whether the community is as safe is another question.

Summary

This chapter presented the role of adult probation both in pretrial matters and in the post-conviction procedures associated with sentencing, beginning with a list of the possible goals of sentencing, followed by the types of sentencing laws used over the years to achieve one or more of those goals. Comparisons were made between the sentencing laws, the ISL and the DSL. The most significant change in sentencing and the PO's role in determining sentencing factors is the *Cunningham* decision of January 2007. Sentencing options in both misdemeanor and felony cases were also summarized. This information on sentencing laws also applies in juvenile procedures.

Probation, as the primary alternative to sentencing, was presented in some detail, including the roles of a probation officer in the adult sentencing process.

References

Abadinsky, Howard. *Probation and Parole: Theory and Practice*, 8th ed. New Jersey: Prentice Hall, 2006.

Byers, Garrick "Realignment," *California Criminal Law, Procedure and Practice*. December 3, 2011. (Garrick Byers is a Senior Defense Attorney with the Fresno County Public Defender's Office.)

Clear, Todd. R. and George F. Cole. *American Corrections*, 6th ed. Belmont, CA: Wadsworth, 2005.

Peoples, Edward E. *Criminal Procedures in California, 3rd edition.* Forestville, CA: Meadow Crest Publishing, 2006.

Peoples, Edward E. *The Development of California's Standards and Training for Corrections Program: A Case Study in Institution Building.* Doctoral dissertation, University of Southern California, 1982.

Case Decisions

Cunningham v. California, No. 05-6551 (2007)

People v. Nguyen, Cal.App.4th (2007)

People v. Tanner 95 CA 3rd 948 (1979)

U.S., ExParte 242 U.S. 27 (1916)

Chapter 3: Adult Probation Supervision

Key Terms and Concepts

Board of Corrections
Case specific supervision
Conditional sentence
County parole
Court probation
Deferred entry of judgment
Expungement
Formal probation
Formal violation

Geographic supervision
Luck of the Draw
Misdemeanor probation
Probation searches
Shock probation
Straight probation
Suspended sentence
Technical violation
3-way search clause

Introduction

This chapter details the nature and scope of adult probation supervision and the roles and responsibilities of the deputy probation officers who work at the street level. It also includes the types, conditions, modifications, and revocation of probation, and the expungement of criminal records. One additional role of a probation officer, that of an acting county parole agent, is discussed as well. This chapter also includes information on the employment standards and exam requirements to work as a deputy probation officer.

Probation Services

The Grant of Probation

Probation is not a sentence.   No one is ever sentenced to probation. It is an alternative to, in lieu of, instead of, a sentence. Loosely translated from the Latin it means "I prove."   Probation is an opportunity for the defendant to prove himself or herself worthy to remain in the community, rather than being sentenced. Probation is defined in §1203 of the Penal Code, as the:

> *suspension of the imposition or execution of a sentence and the order of conditional and revocable release into the community under the supervision of a probation officer*

The legal definition means that, one way or another, there is a suspension of a sentence. The words **imposition** and **execution**, as they are used here, require further explanation. To *impose* a sentence means to give one. Therefore, to suspend the imposition, means that no sentence is given, pending successful completion of probation. If all goes well during the period of probation, it will terminate without the person ever being sentenced. If all does not go well, and the defendant's probation is revoked, then the judge will choose a sentence and impose it.

To *execute* means to carry out. Therefore, when a judge wants to give a sentence, but not have it carried out, pending successful completion of probation, he or she will imposes a sentence, but will suspend the execution of it. If all goes well, the defendant will never have to serve the sentence imposed. However, if probation is revoked, the judge will order that the sentence previously imposed be carried out. The defendant on probation knows how much prison time he or she must serve if probation is revoked.

Two other words in the definition cited above need an explanation, **conditional** and **revocable**. The word *conditional* means that the judge will grant probation, but there will be conditions attached. If the defendant breaks one of the conditions, the judge can find that the defendant is in violation of probation and may revoke probation.

If an adult defendant does not like the conditions required by the judge, the defendant may refuse probation, leaving the judge no alternative but to sentence the person. Consequently, when a defendant accepts probation, he or she freely and voluntarily agrees to abide by the conditions imposed, and not to object when the probation officer enforces them (***People v. Bravo, 1987***).

The meaning of the word *revocable* is self-evident. It means that if probation is revoked, it is taken away, and a sentence will be imposed or a previously imposed sentence will be carried out.

Types of Probation

The probation officer serves as the enforcement arm of the court when the probationer receives **formal probation**. Misdemeanor probation may be granted for a term not to exceed three years. Probation in a felony case may be granted for a term up to whatever the maximum prison term could be, if given, or for five years, whichever term is longer. Usually, it is granted for terms of three to five years.

In granting probation, the judge may order what is called **straight probation**, which is probation straight out of the courtroom and into the community, or **shock probation**, which is probation with some time in jail as a condition of probation. In felony cases, this time may be up to one year, and it still is not considered a sentence. Frequently, the jail time ordered is 30, 60, or 90 days. It is done either to shock the defendant out of continuing in a criminal lifestyle or to punish the defendant for his or her act.

Not all probationers are supervised, particularly those granted **misdemeanor probation**. Unsupervised probation is called either **court probation**, because the probationer is on probation directly to the court, or it is called a **conditional sentence**. As used in the Penal Code, **conditional sentence** means:

> *the suspension of the imposition or execution of a sentence and the order of revocable release into the community subject to conditions established by the court without the supervision of a probation officer*

Note the differences between this type of conditional sentence probation and formal probation.

Conditions of Probation

The conditions ordered with any grant of probation are of two types: standard and special. **Standard conditions** are the requirements that every probationer must follow, such as reporting to the probation officer, obeying all laws, avoiding evil associates, and advising the PO of any change in address or employment.

Special conditions are the requirements uniquely chosen for a particular defendant, or class of defendants. These conditions must be constitutional, reasonably related to the crime or criminality of the defendant, and must be possible to complete within the term of probation.

Special conditions that are frequently ordered include community service work, electronic monitoring, with or without house arrest (confinement), some amount of jail time, the prohibition of possessing gang paraphernalia, or associating with other known gang members, and restitution. Some conditions are mandatory, depending upon the nature of the case, as detailed in the many sub-sections of §1203 PC. As of January 2006, probationers may be required to submit to continuous electronic monitoring by the use of a **Global Positioning System** (GPS).

The most controversial special condition that is often imposed is referred to as a **3-way search clause**. This is a condition in which an offender is ordered to submit his or her person, automobile, or place of residence to search by any peace officer at any time of the day or night (24/7), without a warrant.

In searching a probationer's residence, the PO may search the rooms under the control of the probationer, such as the bedroom, and any common areas shared with others in the residence, such as the kitchen or living room.

If the defendant does not want to walk around for three to five years expecting to be searched at any time, he or she **may refuse** the grant of probation. However, since the alternative is a sentence, which usually is more severe than probation, most defendants accept probation and worry later about abiding by the conditions.

Probation for Non-Violent Drug Possession Offenses

The Substance Abuse and Crime Prevention Act of 2000 became law with the passage of Proposition 36, and is detailed in Penal Code Section 1210 and its various subsections. This procedure is otherwise known as **deferred entry of judgment**, in that any judgment (sentence) is suspended pending successful completion of the treatment program requirements. This law mandates that anyone convicted of a non-violent drug possession offense shall be granted probation, with the imposition of sentence suspended, and incarceration may not be ordered as a condition.

Under this Act, anyone who, within the prior five years, has been convicted of one or more serious or violent felonies listed in Penal Code Sections 667.5 or 1192.7 is excluded from participation. However, this refers to a conviction in criminal court as an adult, and one's juvenile record is not considered (***People v. Westbrook,*** 2002). Anyone granted probation under this law shall be required as a condition of probation to successfully complete an approved drug treatment program, not to exceed twelve months. If the court finds that a probationer has successfully completed the program, and has substantially complied with all other conditions of probation, the court shall set aside the conviction and dismiss the indictment, complaint, or information against the defendant. With certain listed exceptions, the court will deem that the arrest and conviction never occurred. Thereafter, and with certain exceptions, the defendant may respond to any questions about his or her prior record that he or she has never been arrested.

Probation Supervision

Probation officers supervise those granted formal probation by the court in a wide array of relationship situations. The primary goal of supervision is the **protection of society**. This is best achieved by providing the appropriate mixture of **control and treatment**. Control is necessary to protect society by enforcing the conditions of probation ordered by the court. Enforcing these conditions could include searches of the offender's person, car, or residence, restricting the offender's movements in the community, electronic surveillance, chemical testing either on a random or regular basis, and collecting restitution and/or fines or penalty assessment monies.

Treatment is necessary as an effort to help the offender change his or her behavior to lawful conduct and, in the process, to achieve personal fulfillment.

As mentioned in Chapter 1, the probation process can be divided into two basic functions: investigation and supervision. In the supervision unit, officers usually are assigned to perform a single function in order to concentrate their expertise and efforts. For example, caseload supervision might be divided into specialized work units related to offense categories (**case specific supervision**) such as drug diversion, misdemeanor supervision, gang enforcement, sex offender supervision, work furlough from the jail, or an assignment to work out of a domestic violence court or a mental health court. This method of caseload assignment has the advantage of allowing the officer to develop a real expertise in working with specific types of offenders.

In small agencies, officers might be assigned caseloads on a **geographic supervision** basis, and one officer would supervise any and all types of offenders that live within a given area. This has the advantage of allowing the officer to learn of the character and tempo of a given area or neighborhood. The ideal caseload size has been theoretically set at 50, but many officers supervise between 100 and 300 offenders, depending on the type and/or area. With an average of twenty-two working days in a month, how much time can an officer spend in actual contact with the probationer?

In many cases, the probation officer must wear two hats: a **helper** of the probationer, with a goal of establishing rapport and a relationship based on trust, yet an **enforcer**, with a badge and handcuffs, who can arrest the probationer. If the probationer is too trusting and confides some law violation or probation violation, it can result in an arrest. It requires maintaining a delicate balance between the two; to use authority in a constructive way and not as a power trip. If you were a probationer, how much trust and confidence would you extend to your probation officer in this scenario?

There was a time when probation officers were never armed. However, in today's environment, certain officers can be authorized to carry weapons if it is seen as a necessary element of safety in their area of supervision, such as gang enforcement or probation violator apprehension work.

Experienced probation officers, as well as many probationers, know of one aspect of probation work known as the *luck of the draw*. This refers to the fact that sometimes how the offender is supervised and at what level the control *vis-à-vis* help is given, depends on the biases of the officer. Everyone has their biases about things in life, and some let it unduly influence their working with offenders.

The would-be deputy probation officer needs to keep in mind that with a few exceptions, every person the officer supervises is guilty of a crime, be it assault, rape, robbery, burglary, domestic violence, petty theft, or other types of crimes. You, the reader, might now ask yourself what types of crimes do you find personally offensive. Can you supervise a burglar, a car thief, or a pedophile without letting your feelings affect how you relate to the offender? If you can't, perhaps you should consider another line of work.

Most probationers (clients) are ordered to report to the probation officer in writing at least once a month. Report forms are given to the probationer during his or her first meeting with the probation officer. Probation officers often require the client to report periodically in person. However, nothing is more productive than having the probation officer spend time in the field, in the community where the client lives.

Some officers spend most of their working hours out in the field exercising that necessary control and help. They keep their paper work to a minimum. Some officers require routine drug testing on a regular basis, while other officers do testing on a random basis. One officer might arrest the probationer after one *dirty test*, while another officer will provide counseling or refer the offender to some program for assistance after a *dirty test*; or after two or three or four *dirty tests*.

There is a great deal of discretion in probation supervision. What this all implies is that whether an offender succeeds or fails on probation depends to some extent on who is providing the probation supervision, rather than on what the offender does.

Modification of Probation Orders

The conditions of probation are the orders of the court, and, as stated above, it is the responsibility of the probation officer to enforce those orders. However, any of the conditions may be modified or deleted, and others may be added at any time during the period of probation. If the modification favors the probationer by removing some restraints, it can be done easily and often without a hearing.

Examples of this would include deleting a curfew order or an order for drug testing, vacating a fine or restitution order, or changing the time given in shock probation from 90 days to a lesser time or time served.

Violation of Probation

A probationer may be found in violation of probation for two reasons. If he or she violates one of the conditions of probation, but is not arrested for a new crime, it is called a **technical violation**. As an example, if the probationer is on probation for drug use, and a drug test comes back from the lab showing the use of some drug or narcotic, the PO may discuss it with the probationer and reinforce what the judge said about not using drugs, or the PO may arrest the probationer for violating the condition against using drugs and return the probationer to court.

If the probationer is arrested and charged with a new crime, it is called a **formal violation**. In either type of violation matter, the PO will decide whether he or she thinks probation should be modified to add restraints, such as 30 days in jail to dry out, or to revoke probation and have the probationer sentenced. The judge will usually agree with the recommendation. The PO is in a tremendous position of authority in this situation.

A violation hearing is a very formal proceeding. It actually requires a two-stage hearing process: an initial probable cause hearing followed by a revocation hearing, with most of the due process afforded in the original proceedings, short of a jury trial (*Gagnon v. Scarpelli,* **1973**), including the representation of an attorney (*Mempa v. Rhay,* **1967**).

Probation Searches

Deputy probation officers have full authority to stop and search any probationer with a search clause, including their person, that part of their residence under their care and control, and their automobile at any time for any reason, as a part of the PO's supervision responsibilities. Often today, police and probation work together or in a task force approach in making sweep searches of probationers, their vehicles and residences, in crime control efforts. In these situations the authority to search comes from the probation officer and the 3-way search clause. There are times when police officers stop and search probationers on their own.

The U. S. Supreme Court has upheld the authority of any police officer to use a 3-way search probation clause as the basis for an investigatory search as long as there is reasonable suspicion of criminal activity. The totality of the circumstances should be used to judge whether an officer's suspicion is reasonable. However, police must know of the existence and limits of a search clause in advance of any search (*In re* **Jaime P. 2006,** *People v. Robles,* **2000;** *People v. Sanders,* **2003; and** *Samson v. California,* **2006**).

NOTE. Any search, whether by police or probation officers, may not exceed the scope allowed by the search clause. Therefore, it is always better to know of the probation status and of the wording used in the search clause before effecting any search. For example, in a case out of Yolo County, California (*People v. Spence,* **2000**)a defendant named Spence was granted probation, with a search clause, but the wording in the clause limited any searches to a search for stolen property.

Woodland police received a computer generated list of probationers subject to search, but the list did not make any reference to such limitations. Officers conducted a search of Spence's apartment, stating they were looking for drugs, and found drug paraphernalia and some methamphetamine in Spence's bedroom. He was charged with possession and his motion for suppression of the evidence was denied by the trial court. On appeal, the Third District Court of Appeals (DCA) held that the search for drugs was a violation of the probationer's Fourth Amendment protection against unreasonable search and seizure in that the probationer only waived his protection on searches for stolen property. Consequently, the appellate court suppressed the evidence. There was no "good faith" exception allowed here. If the officers had conducted the search for stolen property, and in doing so found drugs, the arrest for possession would have been legal.

If the suspect is on federal probation, police officers probably will not be able to search him or her at all because the scope of the search clause is limited to "a search by any federal probation officer."

Record Expungement

In any case where the probationer has completed the period of probation and fulfilled all the conditions, or has been discharged from probation prior to its full completion, he or she is allowed to apply for a process known as **expungement**.

The probationer is allowed to withdraw his or her plea of guilty or no contest entered at the time of conviction, and to enter a new plea of not guilty. The judge will then dismiss the original complaint or information, and the probationer will no longer have a criminal conviction.

Section 1203.4 PC states that the person

"...shall thereafter be released from all penalties and disabilities resulting from the offense of which he or she has been convicted, except as provided in Section 13555 of the Vehicle Code."

That is, any revocation of a person's driver license is not affected by the expungement of any criminal offenses. The probationer is informed of this when signing his or her initial probation orders.

The probationer has proven himself or herself worthy not only to remain in the community, but to have his or her criminal record cleared; well, almost cleared. Any rights lost because of the conviction are restored. However, he or she must still reveal the facts of the conviction when applying for any public office or with any public agency.

In addition, the code also forever prohibits the person from owning, possessing, or having in his or her custody or control, any firearm capable of being concealed upon the person. Also, §290.1PC states that a person who is convicted of a sex offense for which registration is required under Section 290 will never be relieved from the duty to register under that section.

Post-Release Community Supervision

Pursuant to AB 109, each county Board of Supervisors is required to designate a county agency to be responsible for post-release supervision of non-lifer prison inmates released on what was once called parole, now called **community supervision**.

CDCR must notify counties of an individual's release at least one month prior. Once the individual has been released, CDCR will no longer have jurisdiction over any person who is under **post-release community supervision**. No person shall be returned to prison on a parole revocation except for those life-term offenders who paroled pursuant to Penal Code §3000.1 (Penal Code §3056 states that only these offenders may be returned to state prison). In all counties of note, the Board of Supervisors have designated their probation departments to be responsible for that post-release supervision. Consequently, probation officers now have not only probationers to supervise, but the post-release prison inmates as well.

Careers in Probation

Prior to the 1970s, probation was considered either a drop-out job or a job that one found by chance and took it while waiting for some real career opportunity to open. No one actually planned to enter the field of probation as a career. Many probation officers stumbled into the job by working in a local juvenile hall, while attending college. Many of these majored in sports. They were desirable as juvenile hall counselors because of their size and physical abilities. Once they completed college, or even before completing college, many of these were offered positions within the probation department. It was a natural progression, and they had invaluable experience in working with youth.

There was also a time when adult probation was considered as the step-child of a department, and the juvenile probation division received most of the resources, had the lowest caseloads, and selected the most talented of the officers.

Also, in some departments, an assignment to work in the adult division was viewed as punishment for violating one of the informal rules of the organization or for offending someone in higher places. It was Siberia and once one was sent there, an officer was never heard from again. That might be an exaggeration, but you get the point.

In December 1977, a program titled the Corrections Training Subvention Project, received funding from the California Office of Criminal Justice Planning as seed money to develop a state program or commission for standardization and training of local correctional staff: those who worked in probation, jails, and juvenile halls. Subsequently, **California's Standards and Training for Corrections Program** was established, to be administered by the state's **Board of Corrections (BOC)**, an agency that had long been involved in standardizing procedures and training of local jail staff.

From that point on, probation took on a professional model, with its own standards for entry level positions and for training requirements.

Today, candidates for a job as a county probation officer must complete the exam and 160-hour training requirements specified by the **BOC**, in addition to having a 4-year college degree. Their website with details is found at the end of this chapter.

On the BOC website one can obtain or view a "Candidate Orientation Booklet" offered as preparation for the probation officer exam. An excerpt from that booklet is included below. The exam is based on research and validity testing of the work a probation officer actually does.

Description of the Probation Officer Job

The Probation Officer (PO) investigates and analyzes cases, writes reports and makes recommendations to the courts, enforces orders of the courts, and supervises probationers who are under the jurisdiction of the courts and/or county probation departments. A further role may be to provide services and/or behavioral controls that would aid in the correction of the probationer's behavior and aid them whereby they may make successful adjustments in the community. The major tasks and responsibilities of the PO are summarized below.

Probation Officer Work Activities

1. **Monitoring and Enforcing Compliance** - Monitoring probationers' adherence to the terms of probation, detecting violations, and enforcing compliance. Reviewing relevant probation conditions, such as employment, residence, treatment, payments, etc. Contacting probationers with appropriate frequency, including home or school visits, drug tests, etc. Conducting regular and thorough discussions with parents, relatives, school officials, etc., to check on probationers' conduct and compliance. Setting goals for probationers' treatment or conduct, and monitoring progress. Being alert to signs of problems, anticipating and preventing such problems when possible.

2. **Investigating** - Gathering and learning all relevant case and background information. Obtaining and reviewing appropriate department records, probation files, District Attorney's files, rap sheets, Juvenile Hall logs, police reports, chronological records, etc. Gaining a working knowledge of information in all probationers' files and living situation, including the nature of offenses, prior criminal records, family living situation, and evidence of quality of environment.

3. **Analyzing and Making Recommendations** – Synthesizing and evaluating all relevant information in reaching decisions and recommendations. Making appropriate decisions and recommendations regarding detention, placement, sentencing,

payments, terms and conditions of probation, degree of monitoring and supervision required, and release/revocation. Giving appropriate weight and consideration to all relevant factors in reaching conclusions.

4. **Report Writing and Documentation** – Writing reports (e.g., detention, fitness, presentence, disposition), correspondence and other documents/reports related to intake, progress, detention/ release, etc., that are clear complete, accurate and concise. Adhering to legal and departmental guidelines regarding all paperwork and documentation requirements. Keeping appropriate and accurate records of field and other work activities.

5. **Handling Emergencies** – Working effectively and taking appropriate actions in emergency or crisis situations (e.g., injuries, escapes, fires, physical fights or attacks upon staff). Using *sound judgment and following proper procedures* in using physical force or restraints, enlisting and providing appropriate assistance; and rendering appropriate first aid. This includes demonstrated performance in job simulation exercises and drills. *Note: the focus of this work activity is on judgment and following procedures. Physical ability is not included here (it is to be described later in a separate work activity).*

6. **Interacting/Communicating with Probationers** – Clearly conveying the terms of probation to probationers, including their rights, responsibilities, the nature of probation violations, and the consequences for committing violations. Gaining probationers' cooperation and respect through professionalism, answering questions, providing support and counseling, and offering guidance as appropriate regarding meeting the conditions of probation (e.g., school attendance, urinalysis testing, employment, housing, transportation, treatment, payment schedules, etc.).

7. **Interacting/Communicating with Non-Probationers** – Appropriately and effectively working with affected parties such as parents/guardians, victims, witnesses, employers, teachers, etc. Interviewing family, school officials, etc., regarding

probationers' history, character, and conduct. Providing all necessary information to affected parties regarding court or hearing dates and relevant legal procedures, in a timely and effective manner. Providing warnings to others of potential problems, threats, or dangers. Counseling and assisting victims and family members as appropriate.

8. **Working with Probation Staff and Other Agencies** – Working effectively and professionally with co-workers and with external departments, agencies, and institutions. Informing police of law violations by probationers and assisting in their investigations. Keeping law enforcement, other probation officers, and other correctional and governmental agencies informed when necessary. Referring probationers to medical, mental health, social service, and educational institutions, as needed.

9. **Working with the Justice System** – Filing accurate, complete, and timely legal reports, affidavits, warrant requests, petitions, memoranda, etc., with the courts. Adhering to filing and court appearance procedures and deadlines. Demonstrating professional- ism and effectiveness in providing testimony, participating in detention hearings, recommending sentencing, and in all other interactions with judges, the District Attorney's office, and defense attorneys.

    Maintaining cooperative relationships with attorneys, judges, and court staff.

10. **Performing Physically Demanding Work** – Working with physical skill sufficient to handle emergency situations such as medical emergencies, defending one's self, and pursuing, disarming, subduing and restraining probationers. This includes demonstrated performance in job simulation drills.

Physical Requirements

In addition to the written exam, the BOC recommends the following physical ability requirements for all prospective probationers.

Core Task Requirements Requiring Physical Abilities

1. In the office or field, physically defend themselves (using hands, arms or feet) against an attacking probationer or other individual.

2. In the office or field, physically subdue with the help of others, a resisting or fleeing probationer.

3. Handcuff a non-resisting person.

4. Handcuff a resisting person. (Assistance is typically present when this task is performed.)

5. Run (such as to assist others in an emergency or to get to cover). Note: Running is for a short distance, typically 35-50 yards.

6. Bend, extend and twist their body such as when searching probationers, vehicles and/or placing leg-cuffs or other restraints on a probationer.

7. Put an actively resisting person in the seat of a car. (Assistance is typically present when performing this task.)

8. Use their hands and fingers to search.

9. Using a lifting motion, assist someone from a prone position on the ground to his/her feet (such as handcuffed or moderately incapacitated person).

10. Perform CPR. (This is typically two person CPR.)

11. Walk up a flight of stairs.

12. Run quickly up or down a flight of stairs.

13. Carry objects weighing up to 25 pounds such as boxes of evidence, files, equipment, etc.

Certification as a PO by the BOC requires the candidate to complete a 160-hour probation academy. It is obvious that today probation is achieving a professional identity by developing work-related training and intellectual and physical requirements..

As indicated in an earlier chapter, probation departments are divided into the adult and juvenile divisions, and within each division they are divided into work units administered by PO IV supervisors. Today, the entry level for a county probation officer is PO I, with a promotion to PO II after one or two years. The new deputy usually begins work in a regular supervision unit. The position to PO III is never automatic, but based on merit and the needs of special case assignments.

Job opportunities for the entry level deputy probation officer vary with each county, depending on funding, the crime and/or conviction rate, and staff attrition. The required four year college degree should preferably be in the fields of social or behavioral science or administration of justice. Relevant work experience is the ingredient that sets one prospective job candidate above the rest. The best type of experience traditionally has been, and still is, working as a group supervisor in a local juvenile hall, camp, or ranch. Working as a correctional officer in a jail or state institution is equally acceptable.

Probation departments have the need for individuals who have had experience working with people, preferably in a supervisory or control position.

These are jobs in which one can test his or her mettle, learn to exercise authority in a positive manner, and decide if working with offenders is a suitable job. Many personal qualities come into play when working with people on probation, and in this writer's opinion, honesty and a sense of fairness are the cornerstones of the job.

County Parole

Introduction

When a misdemeanant is sentenced to jail, he or she is eligible for release on **county parole**, usually after serving half the sentence. County parole is administered by a **3-member board of parole commissioners** that each county is required to have. The **County Parole Commission** consists of the sheriff or, in a county with a department of corrections, the director of that department, the chief probation officer, and a third member selected from the public by the presiding judge.

The sheriff and probation officer usually appoint deputies to sit in their places. The County Parole Commission meets from time to time during the month to consider applications for parole. In each case, the

Commission shall notify the sentencing judge, advising him or her of the parole application. The judge may voice his or her feelings about the application and the Commission will give it careful consideration. However, the Commission makes the decision to grant or deny parole.

County Parole Defined

County parole is defined as:

> *the conditional and revocable release from county jail of a sentenced misdemeanant into the community under the supervision of an agent of the County Parole Commission*

As such, it has conditions similar to those imposed on probationers. One such standard condition is that the parolee not leave the county without permission. Other conditions will usually include the 3-way search clause, chemical testing, controls on gang associations, requiring electronic monitoring, and now monitoring by a GPS. A parolee who violates these conditions is subject to arrest as an escaped prisoner. If parole is violated, the parolee returns to jail to serve the remaining portion of his or her original sentence. Parole time does not count toward jail time.

County parole supervision is required by law and is provided by a public officer who works with limited peace officer powers under the direction of the County Parole Commission. Usually, this is a deputy probation officer designated as the county parole agent, who supervises the parole caseload instead of, or in addition to, a probation caseload.

Summary

This chapter first defined probation as an alternative to sentencing, then discussed the various aspects of probation supervision, including the roles that a deputy probation officer is required to perform.

We concluded this chapter with a description of careers in probation, and then a summary of county parole, as a responsibility often assumed by a probation officer as a part of his or her workload.

Reference

Peoples, Edward E. *The Development of California's Standards and Training for Corrections Program: A Case Study in Institution Building.* Doctoral dissertation, University of Southern California, 1982.

Case Decisions

Gagnon v. Scarpelli, 411 U.S. 778 (1973)
In re Jaime P., Ct.App. A107686 (2006)
Mempa v. Rhay, 389 U. S. 128 (1967)
People v. Bravo, 43 Cal. 3d 600 (1987)
People v. Robles, 23 CA 4th 789 (2000)

People v. Sanders, 84 CA 4th 1211 (2003)
People v. Spence, 78 Cal.App.4th 1242 (2000)
People v. Westbrook CA 4th (2002)
People v. Woods, 21 Cal.4th 668 (1999)
Samson v. California, 31 Cal.4th 318 (2006)

Internet References

http://www.appa-net.org/category3.html
Offers an array of web sites showing the various locations of probation agencies in the U. S.

http://www.cdcr.ca.gov/DivisionsBoards/CSA/SelectionStandardsAndTraining.html . This is the BOC standards and training site in which one can find the training and exam requirements for all local correctional officers.

Chapter 4: Jail Custody Services

Key Terms and Concepts

Body cavity search	Inmate safety
Booking	Linear supervision
Classification	Medical prescreening
Custody	Metal detector searches
Detention facility	Modular housing
Detention searches	Patsearches
Direct supervision	Strip searches
Gang affiliation	Validating the legality of arrest

Introduction

Jails in America developed directly from feudal practices in 12ᵗʰ century England in which the local Reeve of the shire (sheriff) was obligated to apprehend and detain individuals accused of breaching the king's peace. Practices in America followed along the lines of tradition, with the sheriff of each county responsible to maintain the jails.

The old Walnut Street Jail, Philadelphia, 1790, from which petty offenders were released into the community during the day in a type of work furlough program.

There are over 3,300 county jails operating in the United States today, and approximately 20 million individuals are booked into jails each year. The states of California and Texas seem to be competing to be the largest jailers in the nation, with California housing approximately 75,000 of these individuals in any given day and Texas with nearly 62,000.

The old San Joaquin County jail, Stockton, CA. Courtesy of California Historical Society

Overcrowding is a major problem, and many jails are increasing in size and staff at every opportunity. However, jail construction seems to follow the theme expressed in Kevin Costner's movie, *Field of Dreams*: "Build it, and they will come." This could also be expressed in a version of Murphy

Relatively new entrance to Sonoma County jail

Law: the jail inmate population will increase to fill the size of the facilities built to hold it.

The old linear style cell block   Overcrowding, with bunks in a dining area
Photos by the author

*Modular housing with single or double cells and a congregate day room in a
northern California jail facility   -   Photos by the author.*

The Jail Population

The jails located in California's 58 counties have a rated capacity of 74,686, but the average daily population in 2005 was 79,639. According to San Bernardino County Sheriff Gary Penrod, law suits have resulted in population caps in twenty counties and an additional dozen counties have imposed population caps on their own jails. As a result, in 2005, "...232,388 individuals avoided incarceration or were released early from jail sentences due solely to lack of jail space (Penrod, 2007)."

In 2006, discussions between officials with the California State Sheriff's Association (CSSA), the State Department of Finance, and the Department of Corrections and Rehabilitation resulted in a proposal by the Governor for a joint construction project, calling for $5 million, to fund construction of detention facilities in selected counties that would house local jail inmates with twelve months to serve and state prison inmates with three years or less to serve. The proposal also included amending state law to require all prisoners sentenced to three years or less to serve it at the local level. As yet, no action has been taken on this proposal.

In 2007, CSSA submitted a proposal for the state to fund the construction of Community Re-Entry Facilities (CRF) throughout the state that would house 36,000 inmates; 18,000 jail commitments and 18,000 prison commitments. Programs would be included to facilitate an inmate's transition back to the community. As yet, no action has been taken on this proposal.

The majority of adults arrested are not taken to jail. Most of those charged with misdemeanors and infractions are cited to appear in court. However, many of those arrested also are delivered to county jails.

With certain exceptions, individuals detained in a county jail fall into two basic inmate categories: **sentenced** and **un-sentenced**. Those who are serving sentences are there for either a misdemeanor, and will be released within a year or a **non-non-non** felony, and may earn half-time credits.

Those who are un-sentenced include a mixture of suspected felons and misdemeanants and, in certain circumstances, those in custody as witnesses, or on other civil matters. There will also be some sentenced felons either waiting transportation to a state institution, or on a state **parole hold**.

For years, most jail populations were fairly well balanced between felony and misdemeanor offenders. This balance has shifted to the point where now approximately eighty percent of the inmates are either charged with, or convicted of, felonies. This increase has a decided impact on the type of jail construction needed, with an increased emphasis on security that requires more expensive housing. It also affects jail classification procedures. Ironically, one current philosophy of jail construction and management stresses open, modular housing, with its direct supervision of inmates, rather than the traditional linear-style cell blocks.

The Adult Corrections Officer's Roles

The responsibility of those staffing the jail is two-fold:

> ➢ **control over** the inmates
> ➢ **safekeeping of** inmates

Within the limits necessary to maintain proper control, individuals do not lose their rights and protections just because they are in jail; and those in custody awaiting trial are considered not guilty of any offense.

In many instances, one correctional officer is placed in charge of fifty inmates in open pods, where the inmates are free to wander about the housing unit, and the corrections officer often wanders among them in **modular style** detention units. This requires a strong and amenable interpersonal style to approaching inmate supervision, as opposed to the authoritarian personality type more suitable in the older linear style jails.

Description of the Adult Corrections Officer's Job

The state **Board of Corrections** has standardized the requirements for county corrections officers. The following is an excerpt from the **BOC**'s adult corrections officer's handbook.

> The Adult Corrections Officer ensures a safe, secure and humane environment for those persons who have been legally incarcerated in local county or city jails. A further role may be to provide services and/or behavioral controls that would aid in the correction of the inmate's behavior and aid them whereby they may be permitted to return to the community.

The major tasks and responsibilities of the corrections officer, according to the BCO, are listed below.

1. **Supervising Inmates** - Monitoring, directing, and controlling the activity of inmates during daily interactions, recreational or leisure time activities, work activities, and activities outside the facility. Enforcing rules and disciplinary actions when appropriate. Adhering to appropriate security procedures when escorting inmates.

2. **Searching and Maintaining Security** - Conducting searches, inspections, and counts (of inmates, visitors, mail, facility, etc.) with thoroughness and accuracy, in a timely manner. Initiating special searches when appropriate. Verifying information and identities, securing evidence, and making security checks. Taking appropriate action in follow-up to searches/ inspections/counts. Safeguarding facility keys and potentially dangerous tools and supplies.

3. **Investigating and Detecting Problems** - Investigating suspicious activities, incidents, and situations. Identifying illegal activity and potentially dangerous conditions (e.g., contraband possession/use, gang conflict, etc.). Taking appropriate steps to prevent problems before they occur. Recognizing signs of health problems, suicide risk, assaults, etc., and taking appropriate action to protect the well-being of inmates.

4. **Report Writing** - Writing reports (e.g., incident, disciplinary, escape, crime, arrest), correspondence, and other narrative reports that are clear, complete, accurate, and concise; writes reports in a timely manner.

5. **Record Keeping** - Accurately completing forms, logs, and inventories necessary for the correct and efficient booking, receiving, and releasing of inmates, operation of a facility, and daily custody of inmates.

6. **Handling Emergencies** - Working effectively and taking appropriate actions in emergency or crisis situations (e.g., injuries, suicide attempts, fires, escapes, rioting, physical fights between inmates or attacks upon staff). Using sound judgment and following proper procedures in using physical force or restraints, sounding and responding to alarms, enlisting and providing appropriate assistance; and rendering appropriate first aid.

7. **Interacting/ Communicating with Inmates** - Explaining rules, policies, expectations, and consequences to inmates. Listening and responding appropriately to questions, concerns, complaints, and requests and providing appropriate assistance in working out problems. Respecting inmates' feelings, rights, and privileges and gaining their cooperation and respect.

8. **Interacting/ Communicating with People External to Staff** - Conferring with the public and personnel external to the agency. Establishing cooperative relations with community, agencies, and other people external to the staff. Dealing with visitors. Responding to inquiries from regulatory agencies, commissions, and the courts.

9. **Working with Internal Staff** - Working cooperatively and effectively with coworkers, supervisors, and internal staff. Following directions and providing assistance, coaching, and support when needed. Keeping staff completely informed regarding inmate status, potential problems, and important shift information. Keeping current on job knowledge and all facility rules, procedures, regulations, and other formal written materials relevant to job performance.

10. **Performing Physically Demanding Work** - Working with physical skill sufficient to handle emergency situations such as medical emergencies, defending one's self, and pursuing, disarming, subduing and restraining inmates.

The BOC provides the initial adult corrections officer training in a 200-hour academy to prepare individuals to fulfill these tasks. Interested parties may access the BOC website for details. This academy is usually offered through the several justice training centers affiliated with their respective community colleges.

Corrections Officer Employment

The standard requirements to apply for employment as an adult corrections officer include a high school diploma, age 21, and the emotional and physical abilities to perform the job. An extensive background investigation is completed before a prospective officer is offered a job, followed by a psychological evaluation, and lie detector test. Candidates should not have any felony or serious misdemeanor offenses in their background. A driving record that indicates problems is a factor as well.

In most counties within California, the jail is operated by the county sheriff. In a few counties, however, the Board of Supervisors have created separate departments of corrections as independent agencies not responsible to the sheriff. Check with your county to determine how the jail is organized. Also, in those counties in which the sheriff operates the jail, the jail is either staffed by corrections officers as a specific job category or by deputy sheriffs. In Marin County, for example, all personnel are hired as sworn deputy sheriffs, and usually must work in the jail division for approximately two years before being eligible to work the street on patrol.

Napa County operates a Department of Corrections separate from the sheriff's department. Sonoma County, on the other hand, has a separate detention division staffed by career corrections officers (not deputies) under the sheriff's department. A similar organization exists for the Los Angeles County Sheriff's Department, the Custody Services Division.

The North County Correctional Facility is a state-of-the-art jail facility, which has enhanced the efficiency of the criminal justice system and is serving the safety needs and concerns of the citizens of Los Angeles County. Important services are provided to the inmates through educational, vocational and counseling programs which are designed to assist in making inmates self-sufficient.

Photo and narrative courtesy of the Los Angeles County Sheriff's Dept. website

Booking Procedures

When a person is first brought into jail after an arrest, he or she is *booked*. This term is derived from the early practice of entering all the relevant information about the person and offense in a large book. Today, computers have replaced the book, but the practice remains relatively the same.

Booking is simply a procedure in which the suspect is photographed, fingerprinted, and relieved of his or her personal property, for which a receipt must be given. The property should be accurately described, but in generic terms so as not to imply some worth or value. If the person is to be detained, he or she is provided with jail clothing, and his or her personal clothing is stored for return upon release.

The receiving or booking officer should verify that the documents that request or command detention or confinement are legal. These will include an abstract of a warrant; a valid probable cause arrest by a peace officer; a valid adult court commitment document; and valid probation or parole arrest and detainer documents; and court commitment documents.

When accepting custody from a peace officer after a probable cause arrest, the booking officer requires the arresting officer, or officer doing the transporting after arrest, to provide a copy of the police arrest report or to complete a proper booking sheet, containing the arrested person's name, age, and offense.

Medical Prescreening of Arrested Persons

Before accepting anyone for booking, the booking officer makes certain that the person to be booked is not in need of immediate medical care or treatment. If immediate treatment is required, the officer will refuse to accept custody and will request that the arresting peace officer take the prisoner to a hospital or medical facility where treatment can be provided before that person is delivered to jail for booking.

The jail intake or custodial person receiving the arrested person should complete a medical questionnaire on each person received. If urgent treatment is required, the person should not be accepted by custody staff. Once custody is accepted, the arresting and/or transporting officer and his or her agency are relieved of any further responsibilities.

Prisoner's Right to Phone Calls

Almost immediately after booking, the suspect is granted the right to communicate with certain individuals in an effort to gain release from jail and/or obtain the assistance of an attorney in answering the charges. In addition, phone calls may be monitored or recorded, if a notice to that effect is posted. Calls to an attorney are privileged, however,

In allowing the phone calls, a peace officer absolutely may not suggest the name of any particular lawyer or bail bond person to call. In addition, the officer may not dial a number for the prisoner. The names of attorneys and bail bond persons are usually posted in the booking area, near the phone from which the prisoner will make his or her other calls.

Required Visits For Inmates

Another legal requirement of custody staff is the obligation to allow jail inmates the right to have visits, as directed by jail policy, by certain types of professionals, including physicians, surgeons, psychiatrists, and often psychologists, along with the attorney of record or one requested by the inmate or his or her family. Visiting must be tightly controlled, especially with family members, and contact visiting is rarely allowed.

Old fashioned visiting via hand phones separated by thick glass
Photos by author

Classification Procedures

As individuals are accepted and booked into jail custody, they may not all be housed together, both for staff and inmate safety and for legal reasons. Each prisoner booked into jail should be evaluated to identify characteristics that can be used in determining where and with whom each may be housed. They should be classified during and/or immediately after booking in order to comply with the law, and to ensure everyone's safety, and to maintain a secure facility. It is the responsibility of custody staff not only to protect each other, but to protect the prisoners from one another as well.

Any classification procedure should be based upon consideration of criminal sophistication, seriousness of the crime charged, presence or absence of assaultive behavior, age, and other criteria that will provide for the safety of the prisoners and staff.

Separation by Class and Gender

Individuals detained in jail pending trial must be housed separately from those convicted and serving a sentence, except for the purpose of participating in supervised activities. Persons committed or detained on a civil process, for example, a witness or a person being punished for contempt of court, should not be mixed with those detained for criminal matters. Diplomats also might require special consideration. Male and female prisoners must be separated at all times, unless they are participating in certain supervised recreational or educational activities.

Separation by Gang Affiliation

The growth of gangs and gang violence is alarming and it is everywhere. It is beyond the scope of this text to present all the details and complexities of the gang phenomenon. Specific gang recognition characteristics and classification requirements are provided to detention personnel in their various corrections academies. Many sub-groups have developed over the years from within these primary gangs, all of which must be identified, classified, and usually separated during detention.

Separation for Inmate Safety

Several categories of prisoners are often separated from the main line inmates because they might need protection from other prisoners. Besides rival gang members, these would include former peace officers and corrections officers who have been arrested; police informants; homosexuals; youthful offenders and other vulnerable prisoners; and certain sex offenders, such as child molesters, exploiters, or pornographers.

Other prisoners might require separation because they pose a threat to their own safety or the safety of others. These would include suicide risks, those with communicable diseases, such as AIDS and hepatitis, injured or sick prisoners, those with mental disorders, and alcoholics or addicts who are detoxing.

In light of the terrorist attacks and activities, occurring in New York on September 11, 2001, those inmates that others might identify with the race or religion of the terrorists might also need protection. Those who are physically or developmentally challenged also need special classification and treatment.

Detention Searches

Patdown and Metal Detector Searches

Pat down and metal detector searches are the **least intrusive** searches performed by corrections officers, and are preferred in cases that present limited risk to officers or to facility safety. These types of searches are performed by corrections officers on misdemeanor and infraction offenders who are booked into jail, but who will soon be released. They also are used in screening visitors to prisoners, and private persons who will be touring a jail facility.

Strip and Body Cavity Searches

Most of the procedures designed to control the behavior of corrections officers came into law as the result of isolated cases of serious abuses by a few officers, or a pattern of complaints about some particular abuse. Corrections officers need to be thoroughly familiar with jail search policies and follow them to the letter.

It was stated in the beginning of this chapter that custody staff have a moral, or ethical, as well as a legal responsibility to protect prisoners and to care for them because they are in the charge of the officers. The legal requirements are detailed in the law; the ethical responsibilities are derived from the professionalism of the job.

Summary

The focus of this chapter has been the requirements of corrections officers when dealing with persons in county detention facilities. It began with a look at jail populations and their increasing demands for bed space and institutional security. The booking process was described, including the responsibility of booking staff to validate the legality of the arrest and/or custody, medical prescreening, and the rights of prisoners to phone calls and selected visits. The prohibition against detention personnel from soliciting for certain attorneys or bail bond people was discussed as well.

The requirements of jail classification were described, to include classification by gender and class, gang affiliation, and for inmate security. The types of detention searches were also described.

This chapter stressed the point that prisoners, when in the custody of custody staff, are in their care. That carries with it the dual responsibility by staff to ensure the safety and protection of the prisoners, as well as the security of the facility. Compliance with all the legal requirements will keep these corrections officers free from criminal prosecution and civil liability, and will assure the fulfillment of their professional responsibilities.

References

Brennan, Tim, and James Austin. "Women in Jails: Classification Issues," Washington, DC: National Institute of Corrections, U. S., 1997.

Collins, William C. "Jail and Prison Legal Issues: An Administrators' Guide," *Jail & Prison Legal Issues*. Am. Jail Association, 2005.

Kerle, Ken. "American Jails: There is a Difference Between Jail & Prison, and It Matters," *American Jails*, 2005.

Moore, Delancey H., "The Complexity of Jail Classification of Gang Members," *American Jails*, March/April 1997, pp. 81-84.

Penrod, Gary. "Joint Prison/Jail Construction Plan," *California Sheriff*, Vol. 22, No. 2, April 2007.

Chapter 5: Prison Development in America

Key Terms and Concepts

Auburn style
Branded
Cherry Hill
Eastern State Penitentiary
Elmira Reformatory
Hulks
Penal colony

Penitentiary
Pennsylvania System
Prison discipline
Separate System
Silent System
Reformatory model
Transportation

Introduction

This chapter provides an historical overview of prison development in America, emphasizing the nature and purpose of institutional confinement and the architectural designs used to ensure maximum custody and control.

Initially, our corrections system mirrored those of England and on the Continent, and included the use of jails and both **corporal** and **capital** punishment. However, as our nation matured so did its penal system to reflect the values and goals of our people. It has not necessarily grown better, only different, and the difference in purpose has fluctuated between **punishment** and **rehabilitation**. The purpose of prison in California until 1976 was rehabilitation. In 1976, the purpose was changed to punishment. However, in 2005, rehabilitation was again added.

Prison Ships and Transportation

An early penal method used in England and France was called **transportation**.   In England, after the American Revolutionary War was ended, English war ships were converted into penal confinement *hulks* – prison ships. The *hulks* were anchored in the harbor and prisoners served their time in them. Often the prisoners were taken ashore during the day to work on various public works projects and were confined in cells on the ships at night. However, by the early and into the mid-1800s, England relied on using a penal sentence to transportation. Sentenced inmates were transported to **penal colonies**, primarily in Australia's Norfolk Island, to serve their time.

British Hulk at dock

Interior of a Hulk

Prisoners huddled on deck during Transportation

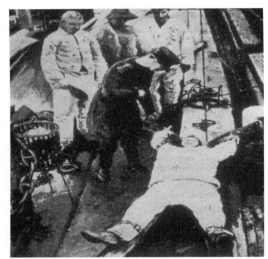
Transported prisoners being branded before going ashore to the penal colony

This inmate population often included women, and children over age 8 years.

The colony of Australia was founded in great measure by penal colony inmates working outside the institution. From 1787 to 1875, approximately 135,000 were transported there. Fifteen percent of them were women and thirty percent of these were married before their sentence. Seventy-five percent were men, mostly single, and a vast majority of them were sentenced to seven years. The reader might recall having heard the expression that someone was **branded a criminal**. Well, as is noted in the one photo above, that expression was derived from the act of branding prisoners before taking them off the ship so that their identities could be assured.

Between 1854 and 1953, the French transported approximately 70,000 men to **Devil's Island**, the penal colony in French Guinea, most of whom died due to the harsh conditions. The colony was closed in 1953 with the help of the United Nations.

The Pennsylvania System

Philadelphia was one of two primary seats of prison development in America. Harsh penalties, including corporal and capital punishments, were often carried out under the British and colonial laws. After America became independent, a group of prominent citizens led by **Benjamin Franklin**, **Dr. Benjamin Rush**, and **The American Friends Society** organized a movement to reform the harsh penal code. The Legislature had been directed to "proceed as soon as might be, to the reform of the penal laws, and invent punishments less sanguinary (bloody) and better proportioned to the various degrees of criminality."

New legislation was passed abolishing many capital crimes and substituting public labor out of the **Walnut Street Jail**, pictured in Chapter 4. However, the public display of convicts on the streets of the city and the disgraceful conditions inside the Walnut Street Jail led to additional reforms. Reformers created the Philadelphia Society for Alleviating the Miseries of Public Prisons, and after a study of jail conditions, recommended solitary confinement at hard labor as an alternative to the prevailing practices.

A small-scale isolation cellblock was built at the Walnut Street Jail, but the Prison Society continued to urge the creation of a large penitentiary system built specifically to separate inmates from one another, and from society. Authorizing legislation was finally passed in 1821, and work began in 1822 on what was to become **Eastern State Penitentiary**. It was nicknamed **Cherry Hill** because, like many builders would do today, a cherry orchard was leveled to make room for the prison's construction. The first inmate arrived in 1829 and the prison was completed in 1836.

The values that operated within the Prison Society were derived from a Quaker philosophy that a person's soul could achieve salvation in a personal and solitary relationship with God. This institution was a place for the individual to do **penance**, thus the name **penitentiary.** Each prisoner was to be provided with a cell from which they would rarely leave and each cell was large enough to be a workplace and have attached a small individual exercise yard. Each cell had central heating, a flush toilet, and a shower bath.

A student's scale model of Cherry Hill

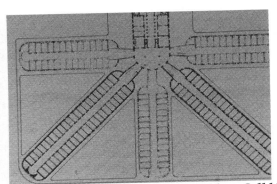

The center reception area of Cherry Hill, with individual cells off a long corridor. Cell blocks extend out like spokes from the hub of a wheel.

The system of 24-hour separation of each prisoner coupled with in-cell feeding, work, and religious instruction, came to be known as the **Pennsylvania System**, also known as the **Separate System**. In 1854 inspectors visited **Cherry Hill** and made the following report:

Pennsylvania, the precursor of all her sister states in the present system of prison discipline, has justified its wisdom before the world in the practical results of its successful administration of this institution. Anticipated evils have failed in their realization. Disease and mental imbecility, so confidently predicted as necessarily incident to separate confinement, have resulted in health and intellectual improvement. Depraved tendencies, characteristic of the convict, have been restrained by the absence of vicious associations, and in the mild teaching of Christianity, the unhappy criminal finds a solace for an involuntary exile from the comforts of social life. He is taught to read and write, and if he has never been blessed with the means of likelihood, he is schooled in a mechanical art which in afterlife may be to him a source of profit and respectability. Employment is not toil nor labor.   He embraces them with alacrity, as contributing to his moral and mental elevation. They help to fill the zodiac of his time, which would otherwise be spent in unavailing complaints, and in fruitless importunity for release. Shut out from a tumultuous world, and separated from those equally guilty with himself, he can indulge his remorse unseen and find ample opportunity for reflection and reformation.

This system might sound harsh in today's culture, but at the time it was intended as a more humane method to treat society's lost souls. Keep the elements of this Separate System in mind when reading about the features of today's prison secure housing units (**SHU**) in a later chapter, particularly those at Pelican Bay State Prison.

After a visit to Cherry Hill, the author Charles Dickens wrote:

> The system here is rigid, strict, and hopeless solitary confinement. I believe it, in its effect to be cruel and wrong….very few men are capable of estimating the immense amount of torture and agony which this dreadful punishment, prolonged for years, inflicts upon the sufferers….I hold this slow and daily tampering with the mysteries of the brain to be immeasurably worse than any torture of the body.

As indicated above, Pennsylvania's Separate System was the product of **Quaker Christianity**. With the Bible and his work, the inmate led a life of simple faith, diligent toil, and moderate habits. Blindfolded upon arrival, he was led to his cell where the blindfold was removed and he remained in his cell until he was released, when he was blindfolded again and led out. The solitary cell and its small exercise yard became his entire world. He never saw another inmate, for even the most fleeting of contacts was considered corrupting. The only person he saw was a religious instructor who made weekly visits to the cell to discuss the weekly biblical readings.

The Auburn System

A very different concept of imprisonment was introduced in New York by men of a different faith, with different views of salvation. They were predominantly of the Congregational, Methodist, and Presbyterian faiths, and they stressed a Spartan life and the belief that hard work is good for the soul. In 1796, the New York Legislature abolished capital punishment except for murder and treason, and authorized the construction of two prisons.

Newgate Prison opened in November 1797 with 54 large cells, each with four double beds, plus a few solitary cells for serious offenders. The penalty in New York for the first petty offense was one year, and three years for the second petty offense. The first felony drew up to 14 years. Between 1797 and 1801, approximately 700 men were committed: 163 for life; 260 for grand larceny, which was stealing $12.50 or more; and 277 for petty theft. Over-crowding soon became a serious problem, and the Governor began pardoning inmates out the back door as new ones entered the front door.

In 1816 a new prison was funded, and the first wing of **Auburn Prison** opened, with 61 solitary cells and 28 congregate night rooms, each holding 8 to 12 inmates. For some reason, Governor Dewitt Clinton saw a value in separating the inmates and in 1821 he ordered Auburn Prison to adopt the **Separate System**. On Christmas eve in 1821, half the population was placed in solitary confinement. It was not long before 80 men went mad.

In 1824 the new Governor, Yates, abandoned the Separate System and initiated the **Silent System**, a system thereafter associated with Auburn Prison. This system included solitary or double celled at night, congregate work in the day, and silence at all times. All inmates had to work in prison industries. Contracts were let out for private industry to establish factories inside the prison and manufacture goods for sale on the open market. Of course, the warden and the prison budget received its share of the profits. In addition to the Silent System, a new warden, Elam Lynds, believed that *"a penitentiary should be a place where everything conspires to punish the guilty."* He was a hard task master and a cruel and severe disciplinarian who used flogging to enforce silence. The elements of the Auburn style of construction included long cell blocks with tiered cells and with the cells off a central hall or congregate area. By 1825 Auburn expanded its cell blocks to 5-tiers high, each block holding 550 cells, and the cell blocks formed the outer walls. Each cell was seven and one half feet long, seven feet high and 3.8 feet wide. There was a reservoir in

Views of Auburn Prison, New York

the center yard for bathing. The public could view the inmates at work from strategic locations for a charge of $.25.

Sing Sing Prison

By 1825 Auburn and Newgate were so crowded that a new prison was necessary. Warden Lynds was chosen to build the new prison using convict labor. A spot was chosen on the top of Mount Pleasant, over-looking the Hudson River near the town of Ossining, and near a granite quarry. By 1828 **Sing Sing** was open, with 513 inmates. **Full silence** was enforced. Inmates had to maintain absolute silence, with down-cast eyes when talking with staff, marched to and from work in **lock-step**, received no visitors, and had no personal effects.

The tiered Auburn/Sing Sing Style   *Inmates with striped uniforms marching*

This Auburn System, with its tiered cells and prison industry, sans the silence, became the dominant style for most prison models to follow. It was less expensive to build than single tier cell blocks, and was easier and cheaper to guard inmates.   Prisons developed in other states along similar lines, but in New York the orientation shifted away from the Silent System to a reformatory model.

Elmira Reformatory

This was to be New York's third Auburn style tight-security prison, but a reform-minded warden was chosen, **Zebulon Brockway**, and he was given a free hand in establishing what has come to be known as the reformatory model. He created a grading plan whereby inmates could earn good time off and eventual release on parole through work, as well as educational and vocational training. Schools at all levels from nearby communities taught all subjects from literacy through college level classes.

Elmira Reformatory, Elmira, New York, 1876

Brockway also eliminated corporal punishment and the striped uniforms.   He also influenced the Legislature to establish the indeterminate sentence, whereby an inmate was sent to prison for a minimum and a maximum, but could earn parole within those limits. **The reformatory model** included:

> ➢ indeterminate sentence
> ➢ education and vocational training
> ➢ emphasis on rehabilitation instead of punishment
> ➢ supervised parole.

Prior to the 1880s, goods were manufactured at the on-site vocational program to sell on the open market. However, union pressure managed to influence the Legislature to limit the sale of prison-made goods to government agencies. This practice holds today in most states, and it is primarily because of union pressures.

Prisons Across the Country

This portion of the chapter is intended merely to offer selected views of prisons in various states, and at the federal level.

U.S. Disciplinary Barracks
Fort Leavenworth, Kansas

Illinois State Prison, Stateville

Fox Lake Institution, campus plan, with family visiting, Fox Lake, Wisconsin

State Prison, Jackson, Michigan

Oregon State Prison, Pendleton, OR

Alcatraz

Alcatraz is included here because it is one of the most noted prisons located in California, and because it is now a federal park open to public visiting. Photos shown were taken by the author in 1973, shortly after a group of American Indians were removed by federal marshals, after occupying the island for about six months, claiming the property as tribal land. After they were removed, and before it became a park, the island was guarded by a few federal officers.

Alcatraz Island

2-Tier Auburn style cell block

Alcatraz opened in 1853 as a fort and military prison. In 1934 it was taken over by the **Federal Bureau of Prisons** and became the maximum lock-up for the Bureau.   It opened with Warden Johnson, a strict disciplinarian, who enforced the Silent System until 1938: no talking, no radio, no paper, one visitor a month, two packs of cigarettes a month, four

View of the warden's house. It is no longer there

A view from a cell to SF skyline

Photos by the author

Movies a year, up at 6:30 am and lock-up in single cells at 5:30 pm. 226 inmates were held in the Auburn style cell blocks at a cost of $10.00 per day, with a staff of 100 guards.

Prisoners at Alcatraz included Robert Stroud, John Dillinger, Al Capone, Pretty Boy Floyd, Bugs Moran, Jack Guzik, Frank Nitti, Tom Pendergast, and George "Machine Gun" Kelly. The articulate Kelly is quoted as follows, after viewing the skyline of San Francisco from his cell:

> Nothing can be worth this, no one knows what it is like to suffer from the intellectual apathy, the pernicious mental scurvy that comes from long privation of all that makes life real.

When Al Capone was transferred to Alcatraz from Atlanta, the Bureau was very concerned that members of organized crime would try a prison break during his transfer. On the day of his transfer, several trains left at the same time going in different directions. When he arrived safely and was placed in his cell at Alcatraz, the warden of Alcatraz wired the warden at Atlanta: "*Crates of furniture received in good condition. Installed. No breakage.*"

Fifty-five families lived on Alcatraz, including the warden, assistant warden and other staff. There was an elementary school on the island. In fact, during my day's tour while taking these photos, I brought a sack lunch and ate it sitting in one of the school's swings. Students for high

The exercise yard

An outer gun tower.

Photos by the author

school had to be boated to the mainland. In addition, staff and all supplies had to be boated from the mainland to the island, including food, water, and gas. It was an enormous expense. The prison was closed in 1963.

Punishing the Deviant Inmates

As stated earlier in this text, every society has a way of punishing those who violate the rules. In the case of prison confinement, the inmates have their own ways to punish other inmates who violate the inmate code, the rules of the informal organization. Their ways often are brutal and terminal, but then the prison environment does not support warm and cordial relations.

Over the years, the formal organization has used various methods to punish deviant inmates and/or to control inmate behavior. Delaware used the whipping post until 1952, allowing trustee inmates to whip

Water torture as punishment

A WHIPPING, NEW CASTLE COUNTY JAIL. 1897

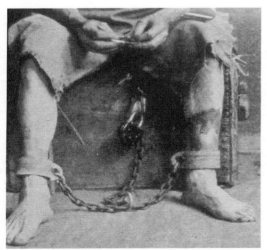

Penology in the south relied on guns, dogs, chains, and cages for road gang custody

behavior problem inmates. When water pressure was available, the inmate would be strapped in place and a hose would be shoved in his mouth and the water turned on until blood came out his nose.

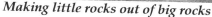

Making little rocks out of big rocks

The flogging room at Sing Sing

Needless to say, punishments were brutal in the early stages of prison development. Corporal punishment is no longer used; it is considered cruel and unusual, a violation of the Eighth Amendment. Apparently, current practices of locking a prisoner in a small isolation cell for 23 hours a day and depriving him of contact with others for years at a time, is not.

Summary

This chapter offered an historical overview of prison development in America, with emphases on the nature and purpose of institutional confinement and on the architectural designs used to ensure maximum custody and control. The Pennsylvania Separate System and the Auburn style, with its Silent System, were emphasized. The Auburn style forms the basis of most prison cell block design today.

Initially, our corrections system mirrored that of practices in England and on the Continent, and included the use of jails and both corporal and capital punishment. Several photos of punishment methods were included as well. It was stated in the introduction that as our nation matured so did its penal system to reflect the values and goals of our people. The notion herein of a maturing system does not mean to imply that it has improved.

References

Clear, Todd R., George Cole, & Michael D. Reisin. *American Corrections.*
Belmont, CA: Wadsworth, 2005.

Lewis, Orlando F. *The Development of American Prisons and Prison
Customs.* Whitefish, MT: Kessinger Publishing, 2005.

McKelvey, Blake. *American Prisons: A History of Good Intentions.*
Montclair, NJ: Patterson Smith, 1977.

McKelvey, Blake. *American Prisons: Social History Prior to 1915.*
Montclair, NJ: Patterson Smith, 1974.

Internet References

http://www.prisonwall.org/cdr.html

http://www.getchwood.com/punishments/curious/index.html

http://www.corpun.com/books5.html
Article about Delaware's *Red Hanna*, the whipping post

http://www.thirdworldtraveler.com/Prison_System/CrimePunish_Pelic
an. html

**http://www.historiansagainstwar.org/resources/torture/brucefranklin.ht
ml**

Chapter 6: California Department of Corrections and Rehabilitation – the Division of Adult Institutions

Key Terms and Concepts

Auburn style	DAI	San Quentin Prison
CDCR	DVI	Telephone pole plan
CMF	Folsom Prison	Tiered cell blocks
CTF	Inmate custody levels	Reception center

Introduction

This chapter introduces the **California Department of Corrections and Rehabilitation (CDCR)**, beginning with the agency's mission, followed by a historical summary of the first few prisons, then an overview of selected prisons and programs. Photos are included wherever appropriate.

The California Department of Corrections and Rehabilitation (CDCR) houses both adult and juvenile offenders and parolees, and supervises them on parole. Many readers might be more familiar with the initials CDC, the California Department of Corrections, the name that agency held for many years. However, effective July 1, 2005, California's Department of Corrections was reorganized to become the Department of Corrections and Rehabilitation, to again reflect a focus on rehabilitation. Within CDCR, the **Division of Adult Institutions (DAI)** is responsible for housing adult felons committed to state prison by the 58 California county courts. The mission of CDCR is:

> to provide an innovative, collaborative environment while maintaining safety and security for the public, staff and inmates. The Division also ensures necessary medical and mental health services are incorporated in the day-to-day operations. In addition, meaningful rehabilitative opportunities are provided through a wide variety of substance abuse, educational, work, vocational and self-help programs.

The mission of CDCR is fraught with a complex array of prison problems and political pressures. When this author taught his first corrections course at San Jose State University, CDC population was just over 17,000 in its thirteen institutions. Today CDCR operates 33 prisons, 38 conservation camps, with over 47,000 employee, and oversees a variety of community corrections facilities.

As of December 1, 2011, CDCR was under court order to reduce its population to 167 percent of design capacity, or to 133,000 inmates. However, it was approximately 15,000 inmates short of that goal. The next deadline is June 27, 2016, when the population must be at 155 percent of design capacity. The last deadline is June 27, 2013, when the population must be at 137.5 of design capacity.

History of CDCR

San Quentin Prison

The discovery of gold in California brought two things: people and crime. By 1850, the state's population was over 90,000. Half of them came to find gold and the other half came to steal from the first half. Crime became especially rampant in and around San Francisco, and the old Spanish jails were inadequate to hold all those arrested and convicted.

Initially a frigate, anchored in San Francisco Bay, was used to house sentenced felons, but that was only a stop-gap in the growing prison population. The **San Francisco Committee of Vigilance** was a prime mover in gaining support in the Legislature to build California's first prison. The state turned the job of construction over to a contractor, who also was to manage the prison.

The contractor chose a site near some clay pits and a granite quarry on **Point San Quentin** in Marin County, and using convict labor from the frigate, erected two buildings, one with forty-eight cells and the other providing rooms for the congregate housing of prisoners. San Quentin Prison opened in July 1852. Within five years over 300 men were crowded into these small quarters, and "…reports of numerous deaths and escapes and of the brutal discipline of the guards prompted the state to assume control (McKelvey, 1977)."

The Governor, Lieutenant Governor, and Secretary of State formed the first board of directors. They appointed a warden and hired contractors to run prison industries. Two additional cell houses were built to house a total of up to 444, but by 1873 the population at San Quentin had reached 915.

San Quentin is arguably the most famous prison in the country, and sits on 432 acres of prime Marin County property. The prison includes a reception center for new commitments, a parole violator unit, general population units, a minimum security work crew unit, and *death row*.

A view of San Quentin Prison approaching from the gate. Gun tower & staff café on left (photo by this author)

One of the Auburn style cell blocks at San Quentin, with five tiers on the left and a gun walk on the right. Photo courtesy of the author.

The reception center was designed for 1,436 inmates, but houses 3,300, and the institution was designed to house a total of 3,317 inmates and now houses 5,967, including the 560 men on death row. The cell houses are built in the **Auburn style**, with tiered cell blocks, but without the Silent System of Auburn.

San Quentin as it looks today. Photo courtesy of CDCR

A rear view of San Quentin Prison. Photo originally in color courtesy of and by Michael Slater, BoatingSF.com

The Death Penalty in California

San Quentin houses all the men on death row. Legal executions were first authorized in California in 1851, under the forerunner to our Penal Code, the Criminal Practices Act. The local sheriffs carried out the executions within their counties. On February 14, 1872, it was authorized in the Penal Code. Finally, in 1893, a law was enacted requiring all executions to occur within the two state prisons that existed at the time, Folsom and San Quentin prisons.

Executions were completed by hanging until 1937, when the Legislature replaced it with the use of the gas chamber, although hanging did continue at San Quentin until 1942. Ninety-two persons were hung at Folsom and 215 were hung at San Quentin. In 1938, a former navy diving bell was installed at San Quentin and converted into the gas chamber. On December 2, 1938, the first two executions (a double execution) were carried out.

The first female was executed by gas in 1941, and the last female was executed in 1962. By 1967, a total of 194 people had been killed in the gas chamber. Other executions were delayed pending the appeal of cases to the U. S. Supreme Court. In 1972, the Court declared that California's

The so-called "death chamber", an old remodeled diving bell

death penalty law was unconstitutionally cruel and unusual punishment, in violation of the Eighth Amendment. One hundred and seven inmates had their sentences changed to life without parole, and were taken off of death row.

The gas chamber, as originally constructed, with two chairs in case of a double execution. Cyanide tablets were lowered into a vat of acid placed under the chair so the fumes could rise. Within about 20 seconds the inmate was unconscious and within about 2 minutes or so, dead.

The law was rewritten, but immediately appealed again. It was again declared unconstitutional in 1976, because it did not allow the defendant to present any evidence in mitigation to challenge the appropriateness of a sentence to death. Sixty-eight more inmates were taken off of death row.

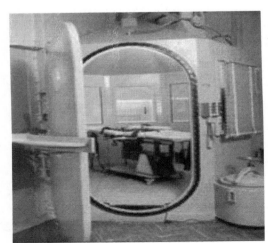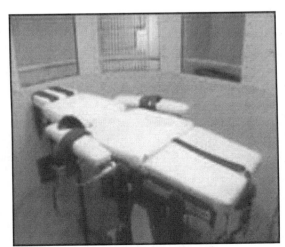

Now the injection chamber   *The Gurney inside the chamber*

The law was again re-written in 1977, and in 1978, it received voter approval with the passage of Proposition 7, allowing the prosecutor to ask for the death penalty in cases of first degree murder, with special circumstances, as listed in the law.

In January 1993, a new law allowed inmates to choose between lethal gas or lethal injection. If the inmate refused to choose, lethal gas was used. Since February 1996, all executions have been carried out by lethal injection, using the old gas chamber now converted into an injection chamber, if you will. In December 2006, a federal judge held that the procedures used by California when administering lethal injections was unconstitutionally cruel and unusual punishment and issued a moratorium of further executions until procedures could be modified. As of January 31, 2007, there were 606 condemned males on San Quentin's death row.

A re-hearing on the moratorium is set for July 2007. In the meantime, state officials are trying to bring the procedures in line with federal mandates. In fact, prison officials secretly began building a new execution facility, with additional room for the media and guests. Construction was to cost $399,000, just under the $400,000 amount for which legislative approval is required. Construction was halted in mid-April 2007, when the building was discovered by members of the Legislature. Their reactions ranged from indignation to outrage, especially since the cost had actually reached $725,000. It is not known as of this writing if or when construction will resume.

CCWF, Photo courtesy of CDCR's website

The 15 women waiting execution are housed at the Central Valley Women's Facility in Chowchilla, shown above.

Folsom Prison

To relieve congestion at San Quentin the prison authorities contracted with the Natomas Company, a mining firm dredging gold in the American River near the town of Folsom, to build a second prison. The state agreed to allow Natomas Company to use

Outside view of original cell block, with thick granite walls

Photo of the inside of original cell house in the Auburn style, with two-tiered double cell blocks. Thick granite walls offer great insulation. In the 1970s, this was the honor block.

Photos by the author.

convict labor to build a dam and a canal near its dredging site, in return for Natomas Company building the prison for the state. This second prison was built on the Auburn style of construction.

The front gate leading into Folsom Prison. Photos by the author.

The inside gate, a closer look. Note the gun arsenal on top.

An aerial view of the entire prison. Note the original cell blocks in the lower portion of the picture, and the 30 foot high granite wall surrounding the facility, Photo courtesy of CDCR.

Folsom Prison opened in 1880. Approximately one-third of the 1,300 convicts crowded into San Quentin were transferred there to maximum security.

Politics entered corrections almost immediately in that each political party wanted control over the appointments of wardens to run the prisons. A compromise was finally reached, and the democrats were given control over San Quentin and the republicans control over Folsom. It is interesting to note that for the next 100 plus years, none of the eleven institutions built were called *prisons*. They were called facilities or institutions. However, the twenty facilities built in recent years are called prisons, reflecting a shift in philosophy.

Two trades were installed at Folsom Prison, with the opening of a jute mill to make burlap bags, and a stone crushing factory to supply the developing highway system. In the 1900s Folsom Prison installed the machinery for stamping automobile license plates. Today, all prison industries are run by a state agency, the **Prison Industry Administration (PIA)**, and in addition to the license plate factory, Folsom now makes the metal highway signs and reflector posts, and offers training in auto body fender repair, auto mechanics, electronics, graphic arts, janitorial, landscape gardening, masonry, mill and cabinet, office services, printing, and shoe repair, as well as providing a variety of educational programs.

This machine was used to stamp out motorist's personalized plates. The inmate running this press carried on a lengthy conversation while stamping out plates, without missing a beat. He seemed to be automated, one with the machine. This photo was taken by the author in the mid-1970s.

According to CDCR, Folsom was originally designed to hold inmates serving long sentences, habitual criminals, and incorrigibles, and it gained the reputation of having a violent and bloody beginning history. Prior to the completion of the granite wall in the 1920's, the prison witnessed

Folsom Prison's "Boot Hill"

numerous escapes; the first one occurred in 1880. The prisoners' attempts to escape took many lives. When completed, Folsom Prison was built with a capacity of 2065.

On the average, 95 percent of the inmates sent to prison return back to our communities. However, many of the inmates at Folsom served such long sentences and were never released, so when they died their bodies were buried at what one could call Folsom's *Boot Hill*, where graves are marked with the inmate's number instead of a name.

Correctional Training Facility (CTF), Soledad

The **Correctional Training Facility (CTF)** is a **three-facility complex** near Soledad, each functioning independently of the others, which opened in 1946, and covers 680 acres. Total custodial staff is approximately 970, with a total inmate population of about 6,000. CTF combines two architectural features in prison construction: (1) the **telephone pole plan,** with its long central corridor and (2) the traditional **Auburn style** of cell block. The South Facility houses Level I (minimum security) inmates, and many of them work outside the complex.

A model of CTF Central, Soledad reflects the basic telephone pole plan, but cells are on the Auburn style   inside

The cell blocks inside CTF, DVI, & CMF are three tiers high within the telephone wings

Correctional Training Facility – Soledad, Courtesy of CDCR

The Central Facility (in the center above) is a training and work-oriented facility. It houses Level II inmates and also includes the institution's **Administrative Segregation (AdSeg) Unit**.

The North Facility houses Level III inmates, and is a training and work-oriented facility that provides comprehensive academic, vocational, and industrial programs.

What is now CTF South dates back to 1946, when it was first utilized as a camp center and was administered by San Quentin Prison. It became CTF, a separate facility in 1951. The Central facility opened in 1958 and CTF North was added in 1984.

In 1996, three dormitories were added: two at the North Facility and one at the South Facility. Industries include a dairy, a textile plant, a warehouse, and training with wood products, silk screen, appliance repair, commercial painting, drafting, dry cleaning, electronic data processing, landscaping and gardening, machine shop, mill and cabinet, plumbing, printing, small engine repair, upholstery, welding, and computer refurbishing.

Deuel Vocational Institute

DVI was named for the late Senator Charles D. Deuel who sponsored legislation establishing the institution near Tracy. The **telephone pole plan** facility opened in 1953 and was expanded in 1959, 1981 and 1993.

Deuel Vocational Institute (DVI), Tracy. Photo by the author.

DVI Tracy

The mission for **Deuel Vocational Institution (DVI)** is two-fold. DVI's primary mission is as a reception center for northern California counties, and houses inmates who come to DVI primarily from 19 northern California county jails. Once the reception and classification process is completed, the inmate is transferred to one of the 33 state prisons where they serve the remainder of their prison sentence. DVI's secondary mission is to provide general population housing to inmates who are serving their prison sentence at DVI.

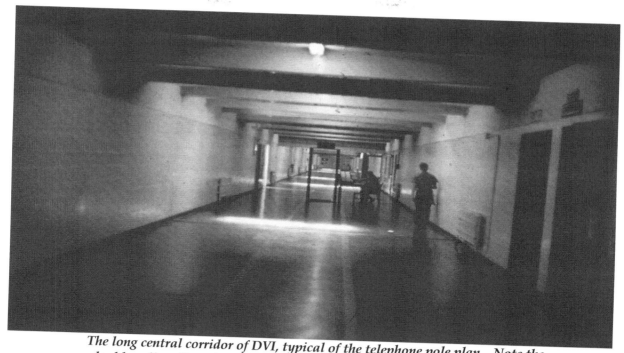

The long central corridor of DVI, typical of the telephone pole plan. Note the double yellow lines down the center for traffic control. Photo by the author.

General population inmates provide support to DVI by working in maintenance jobs, food services and janitorial positions, as well as other jobs that serve in supporting the operation of the prison. Jobs are also available to general population inmates, and assignment jobs at DVI's dairy and in the furniture fabrication, mattress/bedding, and upholstery plants. Academic programs are also offered. Other programs at DVI include Youth Diversion, Religion, Arts in Corrections, Narcotics Anonymous, and Alcoholics Anonymous.

California Medical Facility

The **California Medical Facility (CMF)** was established by the Legislature to provide a centrally-located medical and psychiatric institution for the health care needs of the male felon population in California's prisons. CMF includes a general acute care hospital, in-patient and out-patient psychiatric facilities, a hospice unit for terminally ill inmates, housing and treatment for inmates identified with AIDS/HIV, general population, and other specialized inmate housing. Additionally, the Department of Mental Health operates a licensed, acute care psychiatric hospital within CMF. The telephone pole designed facility was planned for approximately 2,300, and as of December 2005, held

California Medical Facility (CMF), Vacaville, Courtesy of CDCR
Note the Telephone pole plan

3,179 inmates, with a custodial staff of 972 officers. It also has served as a reception center for many years, and for CDCR court diagnostic studies.

Summary

This chapter is intended to introduce the student to the California Department of Corrections and Rehabilitation by a brief look at its history and the structure and role of selected institutions. We noted that the Auburn style is the primary design of cell block construction and four of the institutions initiated the use of the telephone pole plan. When examining any style of construction, one needs to be aware of the type of population to be housed and that custody, control, safety, and economy are the criteria considered in any design.

There is a wealth of information on the internet on the design of correctional institutions, and the following sites are offered merely as a place to begin one's research.

Internet References

http://www.seweb.uci.edu/users/joan/Images/CPRC.pdf
Provides a good report on CA corrections

http://www.cdcr.ca.gov/Visitors/facilities.html
Displays and describes all the CDCR institutions

Chapter 7: CDCR Prison Processes and Roles

Key Terms and Concepts

Bid-and-post system

BCOA

Bus therapy

CCPOA

Conservation camp

Custody levels

Day-for-day credit

Inmate classification

Pelican Bay State Prison

Prison gangs

Prison Industry Authority (PIA)

Recidivist

Secure Housing Unit (SHU)

Valley State Prison for Women

Introduction

This chapter examines the processes and roles within the prison system from two perspectives: those of the inmates and the correctional officers. We begin by looking at the inmate's initial contact with prison during reception and classification. After classification, the inmate is assigned to a particular institution and program to serve time. Photos of selected types of institutional security prisons are included. The prison industries and educational programs are reviewed for these selected institutions. The cost of inmate incarceration is discussed as well.

The roles and responsibilities of the correctional officers are examined, beginning with the recruitment and selection process, then the training academy and the institutional assignments. Salaries and retirement benefits are cited to demonstrate the worth one might find in employment with CDCR, while at the same time noting that these also add to the cost of running the prison system.

The role of the **California Correctional Peace Officers Association (CCPOA)** is discussed as an element of the cost of incarceration, and as the correctional officer's on-the-job representative. Recent prison reform proposals are discussed as well.

Inmate Reception and Classification

Inmates from California's 58 counties come to prison from a very wide range of social backgrounds and levels of criminal sophistication. Some are hardened and violent offenders, while others are nonviolent, immature, and new to the custodial environment. Unfortunately for society, approximately 62 percent of the offenders coming to California's prisons in a given year are parolees whose parole has been revoked by the Parole Board after having previously served time behind bars. They are **recidivists**; return offenders.

The other 38 percent come as a result of new criminal convictions, and these individuals might or might not be sophisticated at coping with the prison culture. The first job of prison staff is to sort through the range of inmates and classify and assign them to the appropriate institutional housing that will minimize the dangers to themselves, to staff, and to other inmates.

Inmate classification is the key to a successful prison experience both for the inmate and the staff. Classification begins when an inmate arrives at one of 14 reception centers located within various prisons. The

Located on 275 acres in the northwest corner of California, Pelican Bay State Prison houses the state's most serious criminal offenders in a secure, safe and disciplined institutional setting. Half the population is housed in maximum-security. The Secure Housing Unit (SHU) is designed for inmates presenting serious management concerns, such as prison gang members and violent maximum custody inmates. As of January 2007, custody staff numbered 950 and inmates numbered 3,301.

process lasts between 60 to 90 days. Initially each inmate is given a medical exam, dental and mental-health screening, a screening for developmental disabilities, and educational testing. Any medical or dental problems are attended to before any institutional placement is made.

The primary factors that affect classification include the inmate's length of sentence, prior record, prior institutional experiences, gang affiliation, level of violence and related conduct, escape record, work related skills, educational level, dental/medical/mental health needs, and parole eligibility. Family location and hardship is also a consideration. Based on the classification system, an inmate is assigned a score from **Level I** through **Level IV**, with the lower number reflecting a need for a lower level of security and control.

Based on an inmate's score, he or she is assigned to one of the state's 33 prisons or 41 camps or to minimum-security facilities with open, dormitory-style housing. The camps house about 4,000 total prisoners, who are typically trained as firefighters. Prison security ranges from fortified **Secure Housing Units (SHUs)**, such as in Pelican Bay pictured above, to low-level security facilities. The chances for participating in education, work, and rehabilitation programs, associating with other inmates, or maintaining family connections, depend on the classification level of I to IV and the facility to which an inmate is assigned.

Prison classification affects not only where inmates will serve time but what their environment will be like where they serve it. Prisoners in a maximum-security prison or unit spend a good part of the day in their cell, have strictly regulated movements, and are surrounded by a secure perimeter with extensive gun coverage. Those confined in a SHU unit for

A two-man cell at San Quentin

Black Mt. Camp near Cazadero

example, spend 23 hours a day in their cell without any outside contact. At the other extreme, inmates in a minimum-security **conservation camp**, will spend a large part of the day out of their dorm and have few restrictions on movement within an unfenced security or work area.

The Prison Industry Authority

Inmates have the opportunity to work or attend school and receive both pay and/or days off of their sentence. Assignment to a lower-security facility will directly affect the amount of money an inmate can earn to draw upon at release, because lower-security facilities allow greater opportunities to participate in work. Inmates can work both in institutional run programs or in quasi-private work programs. The pay of prison work and education assignments can vary greatly. For example, some prisoners work without any pay at all, while those working for the state-run **Prison Industry Authority (PIA)** or for private employers through a program called **Joint Venture Programs** can earn up to half the state's minimum wage.

PIA runs a variety of factories and services at different prisons, and many of the items produced are sold for use by other state agencies. Unfortunately, only about 6,000 prisoners actually participate in PIA programs, and less than 200 inmates are employed by a Joint Venture Program.

According to a 2006 report by the California Policy Research Center of the University of California, Berkeley:

> As of the first quarter of 2005, 53.6% of prisoners were employed and 17.7% were on waiting lists. The remaining 28.7% were considered ineligible (usually for security or health reasons). A housing assignment that prevents an inmate from working will also extend his or her sentence and contribute to overcrowding, because most prisoners ordinarily can reduce the length of their terms by staying out of trouble and having a work assignment. These assignments are broadly defined to include education and vocational training as well as more traditional work that supports the prison's operation, such as gardening, maintenance, or food service.

Most prisoners earn **day-for-day credit**, in which they earn one day off their sentence for each day they have a work assignment. Prisoners who are on a waiting list for an assignment earn one day off for every two days they are unassigned.

Forestry Camps

The California Department of Forestry and Fire Protection (**CDF**) is currently authorized to operate 41 Conservation Camps statewide that house nearly 4,000 inmates and wards. These camps are operated in conjunction with CDCR. Through these cooperative efforts, CDF is authorized to operate 198 fire crews year round. These crews are available to respond to all types of emergencies including wildfires, floods, search and rescues, and earthquakes. When not responding to emergencies, the crews are busy with conservation and community service work projects for state, federal, and local government agencies. Fire crews perform several million hours of emergency response each year, and more on work projects.

Minimum security camp living quarters

A recreation day at camp

A fire crew on the job

Another style of CDF/CDCR camp

The Cost of CDCR Incarceration

Prison incarceration in California is very expensive. It is expensive in terms of the percentage of the state budget that the correctional system consumes *vis-à-vis* education, for example, as well as when considered on a per-inmate basis. Each adult inmate cost California taxpayers approximately $37,000. Part of the reason for the high cost is that California has developed the nation's largest prison population.

According reports by the California Policy Research Center, CDCR has a total of approximately 55,000 employees, with 47,000 employed in institutions, 3,500 in parole, and 4,500 in administration. Of the total, 33,350 are sworn peace officers. Together, they represent about 16% of the State of California's employee pool, making corrections the largest employer in the state Civil Service, and staff salaries and benefits accounts for 70% of the state's total corrections budget.

California Correctional Peace Officers Association

If this salary cited above seems excessive to you, the reader, ask yourself if you will take a job doing life on the installment plan 8 to 12 hours a day, until you retire, under conditions that are confining, dangerous, where you will face the constant possibility of being attacked or taken hostage, work around inmates who frequently carry or have access to knives, pipes, or bits of glass or metal, and who outnumber you six to one. It is no wonder that the **California Correctional Peace Officers Association (CCPOA)** have as a motto that they "**walk the Toughest Beat in the State** ." Also, according to comments by a **CCPOA** member in a Vacaville paper on October 30, 2005, "our members are suffering from dangerously understaffed and overcrowded prisons." A report on the website of the Center for Juvenile and Criminal Justice:

> The California Correctional Peace Officers Association (CCPOA) is a union of workers in the field of corrections. The organization is united behind the mission "to promote and enhance the correctional profession and to protect the welfare of those engaged in corrections."
>
> The union has grown from a fledgling group of fewer than 2500 members in 1978 to a **powerhouse of 31,000 members** who make political contributions totaling $21.9 million dollars a year. The union employs a 91 person staff including 20 full-time attorneys and uses the services of five lobbyists and a team of public relations consultants.

The CCPOA formula for a correctional officer's retirement as of January 1, 2006, is a multiplication factor of 3.0 at 50 years of age (the minimum age for retirement): 3.0 multiplied by the number of years union members have worked for the state is the percentage of their salary they will get at retirement. In other words, correctional officers who retire at age 50 after 20 years on the job will get 60% of their monthly salary during retirement (20 x 3.0). The maximum retirement benefits are 90%, which means that after working for 30 years, correctional officers get 90% of their monthly salary in retirement benefits, for life. Correctional officers are also entitled to additional bonus income for physical fitness, educational incentives, bilingual facility, and rural assignment.

CCPOA Headquarters in Sacramento

Correctional Officer Training and Employment

It should be obvious from the facts cited in the sections above that CDCR offers good opportunities for salary and job benefits. Also, corrections is a growth industry and employees do not expect any downsizing in the near or far future. A job candidate must be age 21 or over, have a high school diploma or GED and have a background free of any felony or serious misdemeanor convictions. The candidate should apply for employment at the prison where he or she intends to work.

Correctional Officers (COs) must complete a sixteen-week, formal, comprehensive training program at the Basic Correctional Officer Academy (**BCOA**), located in Galt, a suburb south of Sacramento. Cadets will attend classes five days a week and must pass all tests in order to graduate from the BCOA. The curriculum consists of 640 hours of training, and ranks among the top three correctional training academies in the country.

The academy uses a combination of academic instruction, physical fitness training, use of force awareness, group interaction, and communication skills. The training program seeks to instill the skills and experience needed to function in a prison setting and to build *ésprit de corps* among the cadets.

Academic courses, or motor skills training include: firearms training, chemical agents, impact weapons training, arrest and control techniques, laws of arrest, constitutional rights of law, rules and concepts of evidence, use of force techniques, process restraint devices, cell and person searches, transportation, and prison gangs.

After graduating from the BCOA, the new correctional officer begins a 40-hour, five-day orientation within the institution of choice. Thereafter he or she is released to a unit or program lieutenant and assigned to a post. He or she is termed an apprentice for the first two years. Post assignments include being assigned to a gun tower, a living unit, or vacation relief or sick leave relief duty. Approximately every two years the officers bid for their post, which could result in a new assignment. Bidding is done by seniority (**bid-and-post system**).

This bidding process does not necessarily mean that an officer must work for years before receiving a favorable post. Some officers have preferences and stay at the same post. For example, a former student of this author, at last report, has worked the day shift on the main gate at San Quentin Prison for over sixteen years, while a friend of this author has worked the night shift in the same gun tower for nearly ten years. There also are opportunities to transfer to another institution, or to move into parole work or institutional counseling.

Valley State Prison for Women (VSPW)

Valley State Prison for Women (VSPW)

Valley State Prison for Women (VSPW) opened in April 1995, and has grown to be one of the largest women's prison in the world, now housing approximately 3,800 inmates from Levels I through Level IV. The prison is situated on approximately 640 acres in California's San Joaquin Valley in Madera County. The current inmate classification is as follows:

Level	Design Capacity	Count
I - IV	1.536	2,980
RC	400	689
Ad/Seg	44	68
SHU	44	73
Total	2,024	3,810

The mission of Valley State Prison for Women (VSPW) is multi-fold. The institution serves as a general population institution providing education and vocational programming for inmates, and as a Special Housing Unit (SHU) for those inmates needing higher management care. VSPW is designed as the hub for female inmates with mobility impairment.

According to the institute's website:

> The institution focuses on providing the general population with work programming that includes Prison Industry, Joint Venture, and academic and vocational opportunities to emphasize self-improvement and to raise their education level. These opportunities empower the inmates to heighten their productivity as citizens of the institution, pave the way for successful re-entry into society, and reduce recidivism. Additionally, a strong emphasis is placed on substance abuse programming, provided in a therapeutic living community, for those inmates with a substance abuse history.

The percentage of women **incarcerated for drug offenses** is approximately 35%, higher than for the male population. VSPW currently provides substance abuse services/counseling to 506 inmates in the Walden House program. Inmates follow a curriculum that includes education and counseling for substance abuse, domestic violence, anger management, conflict resolution, and co-dependency, and includes re-entry planning for those nearing their parole date.

Prison Problems

This section focuses briefly on three problem areas: prison gangs, overcrowding, and a few problems unique to women in prison.

Prison Gangs

It is generally accepted that **prison gangs** present one of the most serious problems within male institutional corrections. Their presence affects the quality of life for both staff and inmates. Inmates want to feel safe, but it is difficult to feel safe in an environment of predators looking for victims. According to the research report *Understanding California Corrections* (Petersilia, 2006), a California official asked a young inmate why he joined a gang. The inmate replied: "I had no choice. I'm an 18-year-old kid. I'm on a Level IV yard. I join a prison gang or my throat is slit." Another inmate concurred, saying: "You have no choice. Welcome to the California Department of Corrections."

The exact number of prison gang members in unknown, and estimates run between 3,500 to 60,000, with the real number being somewhere in between. What began about forty years ago in Folsom Prison over the ownership of a pair of shoes, has blossomed into the most serious situation that prison staff must face.

The California Code of Regulations officially recognizes seven prison gangs, although only six are thought to be currently operating in the state's prison system: the Mexican Mafia, La Nuestra Familia, the Aryan Brotherhood, the Nazi Low Riders, the Northern Structure, and the Black Guerilla Family. California also identifies disruptive groups, which are typically street gangs and include the Crips, Sureños, Norteños, and the Northern Riders.

Almost without exception, prison gangs are formed along racial and ethnic lines. The Mexican Mafia and Nuestra Familia are predominately Latino, African Americans join the Black Guerilla Family, and whites comprise the Aryan Brotherhood and Nazi Low Riders. Gangs are at war with each other and all vie for power within the prison. The two primary strategies CDCR uses to control the gang influence are: (1) bus therapy, and (2) isolation within a SHU, such as is found at Pelican Bay State Prison.

Bus therapy is a strategy in which a gang leader, for example, is constantly on the road, being bussed from prison to prison, and even to prisons out-of-state, and never being allowed to consolidate his power base. The majority of gang leaders, however, find a solitary life within SHU.

Overcrowding

It should be obvious to the reader by now that **overcrowding** is a serious problem and it pervades all the institutions. In most of the prisons, gymnasiums and other indoor recreation areas have been converted into congregate living rooms, with bunk beds doubled or tripled. This creates an environment in which no one, inmates or staff, can feel safe, let alone comfortable; and the need to feel safe can be an all-consuming emotion for many inmates.

Scenes like the one below of Mule Creek State Prison can be found in all the institutions. In fact, the reader can view them on the following web site: *http://www.cdcr.ca.gov/Communications/prisonovercrowding.html*.

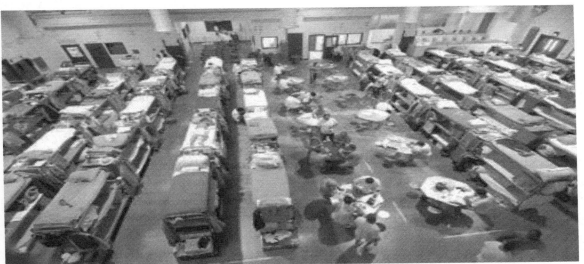

Overcrowding has led to triple-bunking in the gym at Mule Creek State Prison
(July 19, 2006).

Problems for Women

The problems for women in prison are unique. Overcrowding, of course, is serious, but the concern for gang violence or power that predominates male prisons does not prevail in women's prisons.

Approximately 80% of the women are mothers, and a vast majority are single. Maintaining family ties and visiting is a primary concern. Women's prisons are not located near urban areas, where families might live, visiting dress and related restrictions are strict, and overnight or short-term family accommodations are not readily available.

A majority of the correctional officers supervising the female inmates are male, making privacy an issue.

The Plans for Prison Reform

In response to the growing prison crisis of overcrowding and lack of rehabilitation programming, the Legislature met in May 2007, and quickly passed a $7.4 billion construction and reform proposal, which was almost immediately signed by the Governor. The plan calls for the construction of 40,000 new beds for state prison inmates and 13,000 new beds for county jails. To have funding to complete the construction, the state must meet several new requirements, including placing 4,000 inmates into drug treatment programs, increasing the number of inmates in education or vocational programs by ten percent, and creating new facilities designed to help parolees with mental illnesses to stay crime free. The plan also calls for transferring approximately 8,000 inmates to out-of-state prisons.

The Governor would also like to include placing some low-level adult inmates and some juvenile offenders in county facilities rather than state facilities, to allow offenders who pose a minimal public safety risk to serve their sentences closer to their communities and families. This is particularly important for juvenile offenders. In addition, the Governor proposed establishing a sentencing commission to review California's sentencing laws and parole structure and recommend changes, with the goal of dramatically reducing current parole caseloads and allowing the state to designate an additional 200 parole agents to enforce Jessica's Law. *(www.gov.ca.gov/prisonreform)*:

Like any legislation, this one will require time and money to implement, and in the meantime, the commitment rate will continue to increase. The proposals seem to address the major issues of overcrowding and drug treatment. Returning offenders to their local communities will also facilitate family visiting, and it should increase the sense of responsibility of local communities to contribute to the re-socializing of members from within their own communities.

Summary

This chapter examined the processes and roles within the prison system, beginning with the inmate's initial contact with prison during reception and classification, and his or her assignment to a particular institution and program to serve time. Photos of selected types of institutional security prisons were included. The prison industries and educational programs were reviewed for these selected institutions. The cost of inmate incarceration was included as well.

The roles and responsibilities of the correctional officers were examined, beginning with the recruitment and selection process, then the training academy, and the institutional assignments to a post. The role of the California Correctional Peace Officers Association (CCPOA) was discussed as an element of the cost of incarceration and as the correctional officer's on-the-job representative.

The Valley State Women's Prison was described and we suggested that the problems inherent in serving time are different for women and men. The phenomena of prison gangs and overcrowding were presented as the main problems with male institutions. A discussion of prison reform plans was included as well, along with the new supporting legislation.

References

Aday, Ronald H. *Aging Prisoners: Crisis in American Corrections.* Westport, CT: Praeger Publishers, 2003.

Petersilia, Joan. *Understanding California Corrections: A Policy Research Program Report.* Berkeley: University of California, 2006

Internet References

http://www.corr.ca.gov/CareerOpportunities/POR/POIndex.html
Career opportunities in state corrections

http://445.careersite.com/candidate/processcandviewjob?source=folio&
docid=A0303-3382A **Site for CDCR jobs**

http://www.nvccjtc.org/nvccorrections.html
Napa training center for CDCR training, and for probation, juvenile hall, and correctional officer training

http://www.cdc.state.ca.us/CareerOpportunities/HR/CDCR_FAQs.html
Explains how to apply for a state CO job

Chapter 8: Juvenile Court and Probation History

Key Terms and Concepts

AB 3121- the Dixon Bill	Juvenile corrections officer
Age of responsibility	Juvenile hall
Allegations	Petition
At risk youth	Runaway
Beyond control	Status offender
Cross-gender supervision	Ward
Deferred entry of judgment	Wardship
Delinquent	Welfare & Institutions Code
Discretionary release	§ 601 WIC
Home Supervision	§ 602 WIC

Introduction

This chapter offers an overview of juvenile court and probation services, beginning with the legal definitions of two categories of delinquency, and the roles and responsibilities of juvenile probation officers. When one looks at the entire field of corrections, more efforts, resources, and employment opportunities are found within the juvenile system than in adult corrections.

The Age of Responsibility

The juvenile system was created to separate young offenders, who were sensitive to influence and corruption, from the sophisticated and criminally oriented adult offenders. The principle concept underlying juvenile procedures is the **age of responsibility**. That is, at what age is a person responsible for his or her conduct? The answer is, it all depends. It all depends on what the offense is and in what state the juvenile commits the offense (Peoples, 2006).

Today, states vary on their legal distinction between juveniles and adults, for purposes of criminal prosecution. Usually it is between ages sixteen to eighteen years and older. Many states have a minimum age under which an individual is considered either too young or too old to come within the jurisdiction of a juvenile court. California uses the minimum age of eight years and the maximum age of seventeen years.

In addition, all states have provisions by which a juvenile may be found unfit to remain within the juvenile system and may be transferred to adult court to stand criminal trial. Before 1994, no minor age 15 and under in California could be tried as an adult. He or she could not be found fully responsible. Minors age sixteen and seventeen could be tried as adults for certain serious offenses if the juvenile court found them unfit to be treated as juveniles.

California lowered the age from sixteen to fourteen years for certain offenses during the 1994 session of the Legislature, effective January 2, 1995. On March 7, 2000, California voters approved **Proposition 21**, known as the **Gang Violence and Juvenile Crime Prevention Act of 1998**, that substantially changed the nature of juvenile procedures for minors age fourteen years or older, who are accused of committing certain listed felonies.

Today, in cases in which a serious violent felony has occurred, the district attorney can bypass the juvenile court and file criminal charges directly in criminal court. In other cases, the district attorney can request a **fitness hearing** in juvenile court, alleging that the minor is unfit to be treated as a juvenile. The minor has the burden of proving he or she is fit. Otherwise, the court may find the minor unfit and certify the case to adult court.

Categories of Delinquency

There are two civil code sections which define how and why a minor comes within the jurisdiction of juvenile court. Juveniles do not commit crimes, they commit delinquent acts, and as such, they will not have a criminal record.

This civil code is the **Welfare and Institutions Code (WIC),** and it defines and describes two separate categories of juveniles who come within the jurisdiction of the juvenile court. Section 601 WIC describes what is known as the **status offender**; the minor who violates laws prohibiting certain behaviors for individuals of his or her age status. Section 602 WIC describes the real **delinquen**t, the individual who commits an offense that would be a crime if committed by an adult.

Section 601 WIC

Section 601 WIC applies to any person under the age of 18 years who:

➢ is **beyond control or is a runaway**

➢ who violates any **curfew** ordinance based solely on age

➢ is an habitual **truant**

Before 1976, juveniles were arrested and often confined in juvenile halls, and even in state institutions, for committing one of these acts. However today, a 601 may not be detained against his or her will and may not be mixed in any way with 602s. However, one might conclude from reading the current §601 law that it is still an offense for a minor to be **incorrigible**, to **run away**, or to **truant**. It is. However, the court is nearly impotent to enforce its orders because the status offender cannot be detained against his or her will. Consequently, very few juveniles are referred to court as a 601.

In many counties, funded non-profit organizations offer counseling services and/or temporary shelters for runaways. Often there is a fee for services but it is charged on a sliding scale according to one's ability to pay. The enforcement of truancy laws still does not receive the attention it deserves. However, many cities do have anti-loitering and/or curfew statutes that are enforced against juveniles.

Section 602 WIC

Section 602 WIC describes the juvenile law violator as:

➢ Any person who is under the age of 18 years when he violates **any law** of this state or of the United States or any ordinance of any city or county of this state defining crime other than an ordinance establishing a **curfew** based solely on age, is within the jurisdiction of the juvenile court, which may adjudge such person to be a ward of the court

A delinquent then, is **a minor who commits an act that would be a crime if committed by an adult**. The words here are carefully chosen and are unique to the juvenile justice system, and still reflect the **protective philosophy** that has always been the hallmark of juvenile procedures.

Entry into the Juvenile System

Most minors enter the juvenile justice system by virtue of being taken into custody by a local law enforcement officer. Law enforcement have several options after taking a minor into temporary custody (arrest), and in many cases the minor is handled informally and never gets into the formal system. When police decide that a minor should be detained and referred to juvenile court, the officer will deliver the minor to the county juvenile hall.

The Juvenile Hall

Juvenile halls are operated as temporary detention facilities by the juvenile division of a county probation department. It is here, where the 602 minor taken into custody, enters the juvenile justice system. The juvenile hall is a self-contained facility in which a minor may eat, sleep, attend school, recreate, and worship. Almost all the 58 counties in California have juvenile halls to detain minors pending court, or pending placement after court. The populations in these halls ranges from 10 to 15 in one of the rural counties, to a county like Los Angeles which has three halls, each holding approximately 600 to 900 minors at any one time.

Some of the county juvenile halls have what is called a commitment program, where selected minors are sent from court to complete some sort of rehabilitation program. Otherwise, a hall is a place of detention, similar to a jail for adults. Juveniles are booked, detained pending court, or at times pending placement in another type of facility. Those not detained pending court are released, in a sense, on their own recognizance and often under **home supervision**, pending court. The job of the juvenile hall youth supervisors is to maintain custody and control, not to provide rehabilitative services. In the words of one supervisor, their job is, *"to keep them there, and keep them tired."* A tired youth has less energy to cause problems.

The larger the facility, usually the stronger the custody orientation, and the more regimented the programs. Nevertheless, if the reader has any idea of working with juveniles in any capacity, working in a hall as a youth supervisor will provide an invaluable experience and insight into the system.

When a minor is delivered to the hall by law enforcement, he or she is brought in through a secured entry to the central reception area known as **Control**. Once the officer delivers the minor and a police report, and has notified the minor's parents of the custody status, juvenile hall staff accept charge of the minor. He or she will be given an initial patdown search and detained in a holding room, within view of Control, pending a review of the case by a probation intake officer.

Orange County Juvenile Hall

The Warren E. Thornton Youth Center, Sacramento County

Sacramento County Juvenile Justice complex w/ hall & court

Security entry into Sacramento County juvenile hall

Employment Opportunities

The State Board of Corrections (BOC), under its STC Program, discussed in Chapter 4, provides the training and certification of **juvenile corrections officers (JCO)** , just as it does for county jail staff and probation officers. The academy training is 200-hours. Employment in county juvenile halls offers a great opportunity for employment as a JCO both full time and part time. Many college students work part time, or on-call, while completing their education. These **on-call staff** fill in when regular JCOs are on vacation, or off on a day or more of leave. They are often called in to work on a few hours' notice. Those who begin working part time eventually qualify for full time employment.

By way of advice to a would-be on-call JCO, give the supervisor your available hours, always be home during those hours, always answer the phone, and always say "yes," when asked to fill a shift. Soon the calls come more frequently because of your reliability.

The BOC has compiled a job description in order to prepare the necessary training and exams. The following is an excerpt from BOC's material relating to the JCO job requirements.

Description of the Juvenile Corrections Officer Job

The Juvenile Corrections Officer (JCO) ensures a safe, secure and humane environment for those persons who have been legally incarcerated in juvenile detention facilities. A further role may be to provide services and/or behavioral controls that would aid in the correction of the juvenile's behavior and aid them whereby they may be permitted to return to the community. The major tasks and responsibilities of the JCO are listed below.

Juvenile Corrections Officer Work Activities

➢ 1. **Supervising Juveniles** – Monitoring, directing and controlling the activity of juveniles during daily care, recreation, work details, and activities inside and outside the facility. Maintaining appropriate close supervision and security over juveniles to prevent self-injuries, accidents, fights, escapes, and other negative incidents.

➢ 2. **Searching and Maintaining Security** – Conducting searches, inspections, and counts (of juveniles, visitors, mail, facility, etc.) with

➤ thoroughness and accuracy, in a timely manner. Initiating special searches when appropriate. Verifying information and identities, securing evidence, and making security checks.

➤ 3. **Investigating and Detecting Problems** – Investigating suspicious activities, incidents, and situations. Identifying illegal activity and potentially dangerous conditions (e.g., contraband possession/use, gang conflict, etc.). Taking appropriate steps to prevent problems before they occur. Recognizing signs of health problems, suicide risk, assaults, etc., and taking appropriate action to protect the well-being of juveniles.

➤ 4. **Analyzing and Making Recommendations** – Evaluating juvenile records and behavior and making recommendations about their detention, activities, care, and treatment.

➤ 5. **Report Writing** – Writing reports (e.g., incident, evaluation, disciplinary, escape, use of force), correspondence, and other narrative reports that are clear, complete, accurate, and concise; writing reports in a timely manner.

➤ 6. **Record Keeping** – Accurately completing forms, logs, and inventories necessary for the correct and efficient booking, receiving, and releasing of juveniles, operation of a facility, and daily custody of juveniles.

➤ 7. **Handling Emergencies** – Working effectively and taking appropriate actions in emergency or crisis situations (e.g., injuries, suicide attempts, fires, escapes, rioting, physical fights between juveniles or attacks upon staff). Using *sound judgment* and *following proper procedures* in using physical force or restraints, sounding and responding to alarms, enlisting and providing appropriate assistance; and rendering appropriate first aid. This includes demonstrated performance in job simulation exercises and drills.

➤ 8. **Counseling** – Conducting individual and group counseling. Developing treatment plans and goals, and evaluating progress. Providing "on-the-spot" counseling (crisis intervention). Coaching and

➤ encouraging juveniles in volunteer activities and schoolwork; assisting with emotionally distressed, withdrawn, or self-destructive juveniles. Obtaining medical or psychiatric help for juvenile when needed.

➤ 9. **Interacting/Communicating with Juveniles** – Explaining rules, policies, expectations, and consequences to juveniles. Listening and responding appropriately to juveniles' questions, concerns, complaints, and requests and providing appropriate assistance in working out problems. Respecting juveniles' feelings, rights, and privileges and gaining their cooperation and respect.

➤ 10. **Interacting/Communicating with People External to Staff** – Conferring with the public and personnel external to the agency. Establishing cooperative relations with community, agencies, and other people external to the staff. Responding to inquiries from regulatory agencies, commissions, and the courts.

➤ 11. **Working with Internal Staff** – Working cooperatively and effectively with coworkers, supervisors, and other internal staff. Following directions and providing assistance, coaching, and support when needed. Keeping staff completely informed regarding juvenile status, potential problems, and important shift information.

➤ 12. **Performing Physically Demanding Work** – Working with physical skill sufficient to handle emergency situations such as medical emergencies, defending one self, and pursuing, disarming, subduing and restraining juveniles. This includes demonstrated performance in job simulation exercises and drills.

This job description list is comprehensive and shows that the job as a JCO is physically, mentally, and emotionally demanding. It requires maturity, a desire to work with youth, self-confidence, and the ability to use authority in a positive and unbiased manner.

The person who occupies the position of Control is responsible to control and monitor all the movements within the hall and all access to and from the living units. A corrections officer in a county jail performs the same function. Monitoring is accomplished by audio and video surveillance throughout the hall. Staff working within the hall also have electronic methods of contacting Control if problems arise or assistance is needed. Living units are staffed by two or three JCOs and any movement of population is tightly controlled.

A juvenile hall usually has some type of isolation rooms to detain minors who pose a threat to themselves or others. In fact, juveniles who violate hall rules or become a behavior problem are often given some time in isolation, in his or her room, as punishment. "All right kid, you've got 8 hours *ice*." Or, "OK, you've just earned 3 days ice (isolation)."

Trinity County juvenile hall. Individual rooms face inward to the common recreation area. Constant visual contact is always maintained.

The ideal living unit will house approximately 25 minors classified by age and maturity, as well as offense type and potential gang affiliations. It will be staffed by two or more JCOs. However, the ideal is not always attained. The job of a juvenile corrections officer offers an invaluable experience to prepare one for work in probation or parole. It requires the use of authority in a constructive way, and often requires the physical prowess to enforce that authority.

Juvenile Court and Probation Services

Juvenile probation work is organized around the concept of functional specialization, similar to that of adult probation, with the larger organizations having the work divided up into many functional units. Probation officers within these units work for the court, and serve as either the investigative or the enforcement arm of the court, just as they do in adult probation.

The typical juvenile probation department will have at least an Intake Unit, a Court Investigation Unit, a Field Supervision Unit, and a Placement Unit. The larger the organization, the more numerous the work units.

The Role of Intake

The role of the Intake officer initiates the entry of the minor into the justice system. He or she is responsible for making several important decisions. First, **Intake** must advise a minor of his or her Fifth and Sixth Amendment rights. Secondly, Intake must decide if further detention of the minor really is necessary. Juveniles do not have the constitutional right to bail and California is one of about forty states that make no provision for juveniles to bail or to be released on their own recognizance. Consequently, **discretionary release** to a parent or guardian by Intake is the only alternative to the continued detention in a juvenile hall for the minor, pending court.

Intake immediately investigates the circumstances of the minor and the facts surrounding his or her custody and will release the minor, pending further proceedings, to the custody of his or her parent, guardian, or responsible relative unless the welfare and safety of the minor or the safety of the public might be jeopardized. The WIC provides specific guidelines for Intake to follow in making these decisions.

Intake may release a minor if he or she signs an agreement to participate in a form of release called **Home Supervision**. The minor will be released, but with conditions on his or her conduct, and with supervision by a probation officer. The responsibilities of the supervising probation officer are to enforce these conditions and to return the minor to detention if he or she violates any of them. These conditions may include curfew and school attendance, and any other requirements necessary for the protection of the minor or the person or property of others, or to ensure the minor's appearances in court.

If a minor is brought to the hall on a serious offense, Intake will refer the case to the county district attorney (DA) to decide if court action is necessary. Otherwise, Intake may either dismiss the case, place the minor on six months informal supervision, or refer the case to the district attorney with a request for a petition to bring the matter to court.

The Discretion of the District Attorney

The county district attorney is defined under the Government Code as the public prosecutor. He or she is the only public official who can file delinquent **allegations** on behalf of a minor. In juvenile proceedings, the legal document that contains the **allegations** (charges) is called a **petition**. It is also a legal request for the court to declare the minor a ward of the court.

The Petition

The **petition** to declare a minor a ward of the court under §602 WIC is filed by the deputy district attorney assigned to juvenile court. Those familiar with criminal procedures would know that in adult criminal court the DA files a **complaint against** a defendant containing criminal charges. In juvenile procedures the wording is different. The DA files a **petition on behalf of** a minor which contains **allegations** that bring the minor within the description of §602 WIC. The theory behind this is that the court is acting on behalf of the minor as a substitute parent (the court sits in *loco parentis*) and, as such, has the authority to intervene in a minor's life and provide the needed direction toward responsible adulthood.

The petition may be of two types: a non-detention or a detention petition. If the DA files a **non-detention petition**, it will mean that the minor must go to court to face the allegations, but will remain home to await the court date, usually in about thirty days. A **detention petition** means that the minor will go to court, and that the DA wants the minor to remain in the hall, pending court.

The Detention Hearing

If a minor is detained in juvenile hall, the case must be referred to court for a detention hearing. The purpose of a detention hearing is to have the judge, referee, or commissioner **determine if further detention is necessary**, as a check on the DA's decision. The court also may release the minor under **Home Supervision**, with conditions on his or her conduct, or may order the minor detained in the hall.

Juvenile Court Proceedings

Proceedings in juvenile court are **bifurcated**, just as they are in criminal matters. That is, they are divided into two stages, the **adjudication hearing** and the **dispositional hearing**, which are similar to the adult stages of trial and sentencing. California law does not require a jury trial, as do some other states. A judge hears the facts of the case. After the presentation of all the evidence, the judge makes a decision as to whether the allegations in the petition were **proven beyond a reasonable doubt**. This is called a **finding of fact** and is the equivalent to a verdict in an adult trial. The allegations are either **true or not true**. In a sense, this wording moves the juvenile one step back from being held fully responsible.

The Court's Disposition

The purposes of the juvenile court are quite clear: protection and safety of the public, the safety and rehabilitation of the minor, and to impose on the minor a sense of responsibility for his or her own acts. During this period between the two hearings, the case is referred to the probation officer to conduct a social study and prepare a **report (RPO)** for the court, similar to the presentence report prepared in adult sentencing cases. This includes a detailed explanation of the offense, the minor's social and personal background, and a recommendation to the judge as to the appropriate treatment plan.

The Dispositional Hearing

This hearing is usually more informal than the adjudication hearing. The judge controls the proceedings, but he or she must consider all relevant evidence. After considering all the relevant information, the judge will make a **disposition** (sentence) in the case which the law requires to be the **least restrictive alternative**, providing that it is in the best interests of the minor and the community. In approximately eighty-five percent of the cases, the minor will be adjudged a **ward** of the court **(wardship)**, placed on **formal supervised probation**, and placed in the physical custody of a parent or guardian. Any condition must be specifically precise for the probationer to know exactly what is required to do or not to do.

Probation conditions must be reasonably related to the nature of the delinquency, the minor's background, and compelling state interests in the minor's reformation and rehabilitation. If they are, the court may impose any reasonable condition.

Probation

The **minor may not refuse probation** and must accept any conditions imposed (*In re* **Tyrell, 1994**). After all, these proceedings are done on behalf of the minor, not against him or her. A 3-way search condition is usually a standard condition. The court now has legal custody of the minor, but the minor usually will be returned to the physical custody of his or her parents. The court is reluctant to remove a minor from the physical custody of his or her natural parent/s unless home placement is really detrimental to the minor.

If the minor is placed in a **foster home**, the home must be licensed or certified. Usually the same probation conditions will apply and probation supervision will continue. However, supervision might be by a probation officer working in the Placement Unit rather than the regular Supervision Unit. The county must pay for the cost of the minor's placement, although the parents will be ordered to reimburse the county for some portion of that cost based on their ability to pay.

A minor might be placed in a 24-hour residential facility rather than in a foster home. It depends on the needs of the minor and the resources available. This could include some local treatment facility, or an out-of-town or out-of-state residential program. A number of counties place wards in residential programs in Nevada, Arizona, New Mexico, and Utah. The cost for each placement runs between $4,000 to $12,000 per month. This type of care, after the fact, is far more expensive than what early prevention efforts might have cost.

County Camp, Ranch, or School Commitments

Many counties have one or more local ranches, camps, or school programs where minors can be committed for short periods of rehabilitation. These programs vary in size from a single 20-bed probation camp in Sonoma County to approximately twenty 100-bed camps in Los Angeles County. They are usually run by the county probation department, and the minor is on probation during his or her stay at the facility.

A commitment to a ranch, school, or camp is not a final disposition, like an adult sentence would be. Rather, it is ordered as a condition of probation. However, a minor may **not be confined** for any offense longer than an adult could be for the same crime. The juvenile wards are assigned to the caseload of a supervising probation officer, often called the camp/ranch/school officer. The minor will continue under probation supervision in the community upon his or her release from camp until the court decides to terminate its jurisdiction, or until age 21, whichever comes first. As a practical matter, court jurisdiction usually is terminated at age 18.

Camp, ranch, or school programs are usually designed to provide juveniles with both academic and vocational skills, as well as good work habits. Treatment is offered in the form of individual and family counseling to improve the minor's self-esteem within a law-abiding framework. Treatment also tries to provide him or her with the coping skills needed to reintegrate with his or her family, or to be self-sufficient and emancipated.

Frequently, a camp or ranch commitment is the last effort by the court to utilize local resources in an effort to rehabilitate a minor; the disposition of last resort, before a commitment to a state institution.

Caseload Supervision

As stated before, the ideal caseload is 50; however the typical caseload in **general supervision** runs between 70 and 90 juveniles. **Specialized caseloads**, such as gang enforcement, mental health clients, sex offenders, etc. will be smaller, depending upon the county and its budget. Usually, the supervising deputy probation officer (PO) must have direct contact with the minor, his or her parents, and their school at least once per month. Information about each contact is recorded in the minor's file. The progress and/or status of all cases are reviewed by the PO and his or her supervisor on a routine basis, and adjustments in the supervision approach can easily be made.

The PO must be a **self-directed person** who is responsible to manage time and effort without punching a time clock. He or she should be the type of individual who internally can find personal satisfaction knowing that a good job was done today, and not need to seek external approval.

Traditionally, male POs supervise male juveniles and female POs supervise female juveniles. However, some jurisdictions use what is termed **cross-gender supervision**. It would be better in these mixed caseloads for a male and female PO to work together in making joint contacts.

Most juveniles want and need limits, discipline, and accountability, as much as they need praise and support. In many cases, the parent/s of a juvenile court ward are either unwilling or unable to control and guide their child. Often, they wait until the child is sixteen before they attempt to exercise any control, then wonder why the juvenile will not respond to them. Being a deputy probation officer is like being a super-parent. The officer really does sit in *loco parentis*, and must constantly be available for each minor under his or her supervision to provide support, guidance, or discipline as the situation calls for it. How else can the officer show the juvenile that he or she cares?

The probation officer is not only the juvenile's caseworker and substitute parent, he or she is the role model for the juvenile. He or she represents the juvenile justice system to the minor and represents the type of person that the minor should emulate. Consequently, the officer should always be consistent, honest, and fair. The officer also should accept the minor as a valuable person, regardless of what the juvenile has done. What people do is not necessarily who they are. Juveniles do a lot of stupid, impulsive, immature, and illegal things while they are growing up.

Deferred Entry of Judgment

Recent juvenile court law provides a procedure called **deferred entry of judgment** by which the adjudication and dispositional hearings are postponed pending the minor's success or failure to comply with the terms of this alternative program. If the minor qualifies, the normal proceedings are postponed, during which time the minor is under the supervision of the probation officer for a period of between twelve and thirty-six months. Upon successful completion of the probation period, the court will dismiss the petition and will deem that the arrest never occurred. The minor will not have a record. However, the record will be available upon any subsequent referral to court to use in determining if the minor qualifies for a second deferred judgment.

Commitment to the Division of Juvenile Facilities

The state's **Division of Juvenile Facilities (DJF)**, formerly known as the California Youth Authority (CYA), manages the state institutional system for juveniles as a unit of the state's Division of Juvenile Justice, within the Department of Corrections and Rehabilitation. A minor was committed there either because he or she has received all the rehabilitative help that is available at the county level and has failed to reform (so the expression goes), or because the present offense and/or delinquent orientation of the minor poses an immediate threat to the community.

Counties are no longer committing juveniles to state facilities, except in serious cases, and are making every effort to use local resources for juvenile rehabilitation rather than commit them to the state institutions because of the lack of services provided to youth by the state. By July 2014, the DJF will cease to exist and all juvenile offenders will be retained at the local level.

Summary

This chapter summarized the workings of juvenile court and the functions of probation during and after the court process. The role of juvenile hall and the JCO were detailed, and employment in a juvenile hall was offered as a good career and as a great experience to prepare one to work in probation. A detailed job description of the JCO, and the required 200-hour training academy, were detailed as well.

References

Peoples, Edward E. *Juvenile Procedures in California*, 4th edition Forestville, CA: Meadow Crest Publishing, 2006

Case Decision

In re Tyrell, 8 CA 4th 68 (1994)

Chapter 9: The State Division of Juvenile Facilities

Key Terms and Concepts

California Youth Authority

DSL commitment time

Division of Juvenile Facilities (DJF)

Maximum confinement time

Offense Baseline Chart

Parole consideration date (PCD)

Reception center

270 ° plan

Introduction

This chapter focuses entirely on the **Division of Juvenile Facilities**, **(DJF)**, previously known as the California Youth Authority **(CYA)**. It is the state organization that administers the institutions and parole services for young offenders. It is similar to the prison and parole services given adults committed to the California Department of Corrections and Rehabilitation (CDCR).

Originally, CDCR and CYA were organizational divisions of the state's Youth and Adult Correctional Agency, who's Secretary reported directly to the Governor. However, legislation in 2005 reorganized these agencies into the Department of Corrections and Rehabilitation, with a Division of Adult Services, and the Division of Juvenile Services. Within the Division of Juvenile Services are a Division of Juvenile Facilities and the Division of Juvenile Justice Parole Operations. As stated, this chapter is concerned with the Division of Juvenile Facilities.

Protection of society is DJF's primary purpose. However, that protection is to be accomplished through rehabilitative services for youthful offenders. DJF is also heavily involved in providing delinquency prevention programs throughout the state as well, and in assisting local agencies with resources and training.

A Brief History of the California Youth Authority

CYA (DJF) is only sixty-six years old, but its roots are imbedded in California's initial efforts to develop a reform school system, some of which was mentioned in Chapter 1.

The first steps were taken when the San Francisco Industrial School was established by the Legislature on May 5, 1859, with a capacity for forty-eight boys and girls ages 13 to 18 years. Juveniles of maturity beyond their years were housed in San Quentin. In 1860 the State Reform School of Marysville opened, but it was closed in 1868 because of low population. The twenty-eight boys committed there were transferred to the San Francisco Industrial School, and the state agreed to pay $15 in gold coin per month for each child detained. In 1868, the girls in the San Francisco Industrial School were transferred to the Magdelen Asylum in San Francisco.

In 1875 the training ship *Jamestown* was transferred from the Navy to the City of San Francisco to supplement the Industrial School as a place of commitment for boys. They were given training in seamanship and navigation, and after six months were eligible for employment as seamen on merchant ships. Within four years, however, the ship was returned to the Navy due to mismanagement and complaints that the *Jamestown* was really a training ship for criminals.

The need for placement facilities for juveniles continued to grow, and most people wanted to have juveniles completely separate from adults. Finally, in 1890 the Legislature enacted a law establishing a state reform school system, and by 1892 the San Francisco Industrial School was closed. The Whittier State Reformatory for Boys and Girls opened in 1891 with 300 youths, and Preston School of Industry (aka *The Castle*) opened to

Preston School of Industry, aka "The Castle"

house the older boys in 1895. By 1907, all youths under age 18 were transferred from San Quentin to these reform schools. By 1913, girls were separated from boys and were transferred from Whittier to the new Ventura School for Girls.

The California Youth Authority was established by law in 1941, to accept all court commitments under the age of 23 years. In 1943, the Governor transferred to CYA the management of California's existing reform schools: Preston School of Industry in Ione, the Whittier School for Boys (re-named the Fred C. Nelles School for Boys), and the Ventura School for Girls. The total ward population at the time was 1,080 in the institutions and 1,625 on parole.

Over the years, CYA grew considerably larger.   In 1943, it transferred fifty boys from various county jails to the Calaveras Big Tree Park, where they built a 100-bed camp. In that same year, CYA purchased the Knights of Pythias Old Peoples' Home and Orphanage off Highway 12, in rural Sonoma County, renovated the grounds and buildings, and opened the **Los Guilicos School for Girls**. **Fricot Ranch School**, a camp-like setting for young boys in the Sierra foothills, opened in 1944. These facilities were insufficient to house all the young commitments awaiting delivery to CYA. Many were detained in local juvenile halls, county jails, and on two army bases. **Over-crowding** was as much a problem then as now.

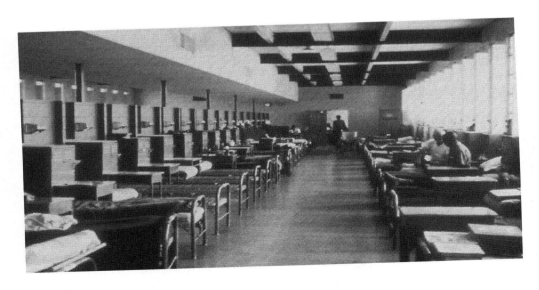

Dorm living at Camp Ben Lomond (Photo by the author)

At the close of World War II, the army-based juvenile camps were closed, but there was still a need for new facilities. The Legislature responded by authorizing additional institutions. The California Vocational Institution at Lancaster was opened for older boys in 1945. Pine Grove Camp opened in 1945, and Camp Ben Lomond opened in 1947. Also in 1947, the Paso Robles School for Boys opened on a 200 acre abandoned army base with 40 barracks. Commitments to CYA continued to increase. In 1954, a **reception center** and clinic was opened in Perkins (now a part of Sacramento) in the northern part of the state, and at the Norwalk Clinic, in the south. Mt. Bullion Camp opened in 1956 near Mariposa; the Youth Training Center (YTC) opened in Ontario in 1960; and Washington Ridge Camp near Nevada City opened in 1961. Additional camps were opened in 1972 and 1979.

The California Youth Authority was given departmental status in 1953, and in 1961, it became a part of the Youth and Adult Corrections Agency, along with the California Department of Corrections (CDC).

In 1964, a **reception center** and clinic for girls was opened at the Ventura School for Girls, leaving the Norwalk Clinic exclusively for boys. The Northern California Youth Center (NCYC) opened in 1965, on the southern edge of Stockton. The original plans for NCYC called for twelve 400-bed facilities clustered around a central administrative center. Each facility was to have four two-wing units, with the wings separated by a staff office, and dorm-style living for 50 boys in each wing.

To date, only four of the twelve planned facilities have been opened: O. H. Close School for Boys in 1966; Karl Holton School for Boys in 1967; Dewitt Nelson School for Boys in 1971; and the N. A. Chaderjian School in 1991.

Housing in the first three institutions is of the dorm-style, reflecting an open environment, while that of the Chaderjian School uses the so-called **270° plan**, in which large square housing buildings are divided inside into two or more quads by walls. Supervising staff sits in a tower-like room positioned above the quads, giving them 270 degrees of vision, while the cell-like rooms ring the perimeter of each quad. Other staff work on the floors below.

The growth of CYA's population slowed, and even declined, in the late 1960s and 1970s, with the implementation of a probation subsidy program and the law change eliminating the juvenile commitment for status offenses.

In fact, several institutions, such as the Fricot School and Los Guilicos School, were closed and sold when it appeared that California had found the magic solution to treating delinquents. However, with the demise of the probation subsidy, the increase in violent offenses by juveniles, and a get-tough attitude toward delinquents, the magic solution evaporated and the institutional population soared to a record level.

Institutions were expanded and new ones built, with the Herman G. Stark Youth Training School in Chino and the above-mentioned Chaderjian Correctional Facility in Stockton, among the most recently built. DJF now has eleven institutions and four forestry camps and operates today at approximately 120 percent capacity. However, the ward population has been declining in recent years, with the passage of Proposition 21 because an increasing number of youths are certified to adult court to face criminal prosecution.

DJF's Population Profile

For many years, DJF operated the largest youthful offender program in the nation, and probably in the world. However, the population has shown a dramatic decrease over the past ten years.

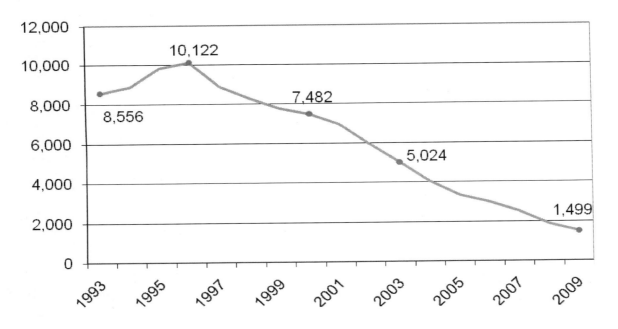

Population of CYA, 1993-2009

DJF's population runs between ages 12 and 25 years. It is composed of commitments from **three sources**:

➤ juvenile court commitments

➤ adults convicted in criminal court but committed to the Division of Juvenile Facilities instead of prison

➤ adults convicted of crimes and sentenced to prison, but ordered to be confined in a DJF facility because of a young age or immaturity

DJF Programs

Within the institutions, two institution-based camps, Los Robles at El Paso de Robles (Paso Robles), and the Carraway Fire and Public Service Camp in Stockton, provide extensive training for males in fighting forest fires and doing soil and forest conservation work. The Ventura Youth Correctional Facility provides similar training for females. Wards are also trained in fire-fighting and soil and forest conservation at the Preston and Stark facilities.

It is interesting to note that in the year 2000, all the Youth Authority institutions were named "Schools". Now, seven years later, many have been re-named a "Correctional Facility". Some facilities, such as O. H. Close in Stockton and Fred C. Nelles in Whittier, stress education,

Dorm living unit, Karl Holton School, Stockton (photo by the author)

and prepare wards to receive a high school diploma or GED. College credits are earned through local colleges and universities. Other institutions focus on vocational training, in cooperation with private industry, such as auto mechanics, culinary arts, horticulture, and computer programming, to name but a few. It is also interesting to note that when this author visited the Stockton facilities several times during the 1970s and 1980s, there was no uniformed staff. The dorm youth supervisors wore casual clothes and security wore gray slacks and blue blazers. Today, most staff wear the olive colored corrections officers uniforms.

Living unit day room at Karl Holton (photo by the author)

The open inner yards within the O. H. Close Stockton facilities

In 2004, CDCR established the Herman G. Stark Youth Training School for the confinement of juvenile males convicted as adults in criminal court. It was designed as an intermediate security institution to provide custody and care, industrial, vocational, and other training, guidance and reformatory help for young men, too mature to benefit from schools for juveniles, and too immature for confinement in prisons.

The inner yard of Stockton Facility, with circular track

Security in the school area where main control cannot view

The control station of O.H. Close with visual and/or audio contact throughout the facility. All wards' movements are controlled by staff (Photo by the author)

Specialized Programs

In addition to the basic academic and vocational programs, DJF offers an array of specialized programs to meet the treatment needs of the wards:

➤ Drug and Alcohol Abuse Formalized Treatment

➤ Fire Suppression and Public Service Camps

➤ Medical/Psychiatric-Intensive Treatment

➤ Non-Violent Offender Treatment

➤ Parole Violator Program

➤ Planned Re-Entry Program (PREP)

➤ Pre-Camp Training

➤ Psychiatric Hospitalization

➤ Sex Offender Treatment

➤ Work Experience/Youth Services

The Cost of DJF

The cost of committing juveniles to DJF is very high. For the fiscal year 2004, DJF reported that the *per capita* cost for each ward was $80,000. When one considers that the average length of stay is 28 months, the cost for each ward averages almost approximately $186,000. This begs the question: What could have been done for the juvenile within the family or community with that much money?

The DJF Commitment: Calculating the Commitment Time

A shift from treatment to punishment is evident in the way the court's authority has changed in recent years. Before 1982, a minor could be committed to a local ranch or camp or to DJF for an indefinite period, up to the age at which legal jurisdiction would end, age 21 years, or in some cases, age 25. Now, however, a juvenile may not receive more commitment time in any type of secure facility than an adult could receive as a criminal sentence, regardless of the minor's treatment needs (see, *In re Bryant R., 2003*). This limits misdemeanor commitments to either six months or one year, and felony commitments to whatever time the Penal Code provides for adult sentences.

The Welfare and Institutions Code authorizes a judge to commit a minor to the DJF, but the judge must refer to the Penal Code and follow the sentencing procedures and guidelines of the adult **Determinate Sentence Law (DSL)** established by the Legislature, as provided in Penal Code Section 1170.

Oddly enough, the U. S. Supreme Court's *Cunningham* decision of January 2007 (discussed in Chapter 2) in which the Court found the existing DSL unconstitutional, does not affect the juvenile court's commitment procedures. Since there is no jury in juvenile court, the judge hears a delinquent case sitting alone. Consequently, he or she hears and considers the factors in mitigation and aggravation. and can choose any of the three DSL times the law allows. That does not mean that the juvenile will remain incarcerated for that length of time.

The time the judge chooses sets what is termed the **maximum confinement time** that a juvenile may be detained in DJF for treatment. After the ward arrives at DJF, the Board of Parole Hearings (Parole Board) determines the actual program time that the juvenile will be confined before being released on parole.

DJF Reception and Placement

When a minor is committed to DJF, he or she is sent initially to one of the reception centers where he or she undergoes a 45 to 60 day period of diagnostic study and evaluation. This includes educational and psychological testing, medical and dental examinations, and an assessment of the minor's background and treatment needs. A report is prepared, with a recommendation as to what programming would benefit the minor.

The Board of Parole Hearings meets and reviews the evaluation report, and decides whether the minor can benefit from the rehabilitative programs available at DJF. If the Board accepts the commitment, it sets a **maximum confinement time**, which also sets a parole consideration date (PCD). The time selected is derived from an **offense baseline chart** detailed in the California Administrative Code, a separate series of guidelines the Board uses to determine an appropriate confinement time for a minor.

Institutional Lockups and Restraints

There is an old axiom which holds that every society has a way of punishing the deviant, whether that refers to our large society, the social grouping within an organization, or the micro-society within an institution. There needs to be a way to control and/or isolate those who disrupt the norm; or as the institutional expression goes, *who don't adjust to the program.*

Corrections officers have ready access to a variety of restraints, such as handcuffs, mace, strait jackets, and lockups, or isolation rooms. The two photos above were taken in the mid-1970s by the author during student tours of the facilities. Barely visible are the steel bar doors inside the outside doors at the Karl Holton School isolation unit.

The doors of the rooms in the Preston isolation unit had a round hole about head high, with a swivel cover that could be opened to allow the

Isolation unit in the old Preston School   Isolation unit in Karl Holton School

insert of a tear gas gun. This was used if a ward was still a behavior problem once locked up. We were told that after thirty minutes in a small room filled with tear gas, the juvenile was more amenable to direction.

Within the C. J. Chaderjian facility in Stockton, wards often are locked in their rooms for twenty-two hours a day. A state report in 2004 showed that conditions at Chaderjian were so bad that one senator recommended completely closing down the DJF. However Governor Schwarzenegger, in response to a class action suit, promised to improve conditions.

A report of February 2007, by the state's Inspector General showed that conditions at the DJF's Chino facility were as bad as they were at Chaderjian, and created an environment conducive to violence and suicide by wards. "Nothing has changed," responded Senate Majority Leader, Gloria Romero, "We're dealing with an organization that is impervious to change (*SF Chronicle*, Feb. 28, 2007)." Reforms should come quickly from within DJF or they will be imposed from without by a federal court.

Employment Opportunities

There are two categories of correctional work available with DJF: the **Youth Corrections Officer (YCO)** and the **Youth Corrections Counselor (YCC).** The YCO is the entry level position as a peace officer within the institutions. They are responsible for protecting the public, other staff, and wards in a multitude of areas inside and outside the facilities. According to DJF, the job of YCO, "offers an individual the opportunity to grow, a different challenge each day, and a feeling of accomplishment." Minimum qualifications to apply for the job are:

- no felony convictions
- be a U.S. citizen or a permanent resident alien who is eligible to apply for citizenship prior to completing the background investigation
- high school graduate or GED
- a history of law abiding behavior (this is critical)
- be at least 20 ½ years of age

The position of **Youth Corrections Counselor** offers individuals the opportunity to assume a more treatment orientation rather than one of custody. The basic requirements are the same as for the YCO, but in addition the applicant must have either a four-year college or university degree or sixty semester hours plus two years paid job experience working with youth. An excellent employment path to follow would be to work as a YCO for two or more years, obtain a college degree, then apply for the YCC position. A good thing to keep in mind when working on one job is that you are auditioning for the next job.

An individual hired as either a YCO or YCC will complete the corrections officers' basic academy at the Galt campus.

Summary

This chapter focused entirely on the Division of Juvenile Facilities, the state organization that administers the institutional services for young offenders. The array of institutional services and programs were detailed. The role of the Board of Parole Hearings in setting the actual confinement time for a minor was mentioned, but the actual parole process is covered in Chapter 10. It was noted that the Board is the primary controlling authority for all activities, programs, and commitment time, experienced by the wards.

References

Peoples, Edward E. *Juvenile Procedures in California, 4ᵗʰ ed.* Forestville: Meadow Crest Publishing, 2006

Martin, Mark. "Grim Conditions at Youth Prison," *San Francisce Chronicle*, Feb. 28, 2007

Internet References

http://www.nccd-crc.org/nccd/dnld/Home/A_New_Era.pdf

http://www.cya.ca.gov/
http://www.cya.ca.gov/CareerOpportunities/POR/PeaceOfficer_Index. html

Case Decision

In re Bryant R. CA 4ᵗʰ (No. F041423) (2003)

Chapter 10: State Parole

Key Terms and Concepts

Alexander Maconochie	Irish System
Board of Parole Hearings	Mandatory release
Discretionary release	Mark System
Gate money	Parole
High control parolee	Placement plan
Honorable discharge	Regular supervision
Indeterminate sentence	Sir Walter Crofton
Intensive re-entry	Ticket-of-leave

Introduction

This chapter combines **adult parole** and **juvenile parole** into one presentation because one state agency handles all parole matters within California. Nevertheless, the chapter is divided into two sections: one for adult parole and one for juvenile parole. As was stated in Chapter 5, The California Department of Corrections and Rehabilitation (CDCR) is the umbrella agency that is responsible for both adult and juvenile institutional offenders and parolees. Within CDCR there is only one parole board, the **Board of Parole Hearings**.

The processes for adult and juvenile parole are examined and similarities and differences between the two are cited. The chapter begins with a brief history of parole practices.

Origins of Parole

The Mark System

The sources of parole from European practices are many and varied. One such noted source was the efforts of Captain **Alexander Maconochie**, a former Professor of Geography at the University of London, who was appointed to administer England's new penal colony of Norfolk Island, Australia in 1840. He wanted to shift the focus of penology from punishment to reform. He argued that an inmate's correction (after transportation) should have two dimensions: punishment for his past and training with incentives for his future. He argued that sentences should be indeterminate, and that the convicts should have to earn a certain number of credits or marks, for good behavior and hard work, before they were released. This was termed the **Mark System.**

Marks could be exchanged for either goods or time. The prisoner could buy "luxuries" with his marks, such as extra food, tobacco, and clothing. Ideally, the convict would pay for everything beyond a diet of bread and water with the marks he earned. Maconochie believed that: "THE FATE OF EVERY MAN SHOULD BE PLACED UNRESERVEDLY IN HIS OWN HANDS...THERE SHOULD BE NO FAVOUR ANYWHERE."

Alexander Maconochie

Upon arrival at Norfolk Island penal colony, he had all the inmates line up in the yard. He then walked with his wife and two children through the yard to the gallows, where all watched as the gallows was dismantled. He stopped the use of the special double-loaded cats-o'-nine tails used to flog convicts for breaking rules. He also learned the names of each convict and called them by name.

In this Mark System, convicts would buy their way out of prison with these marks. To buy, they had to save and prioritize how they wanted to spend their earned marks. In a sense this was training the convicts in capitalism and social responsibility, and leaving the length of the sentence up to the convict himself. Anyone researching the treatment approach called behavior modification, used extensively by the California Youth Authority during the 1960s and 1970s, will find its source in Maconochie's Mark System.

As soon as a convict entered the penal colony, he would begin with a short harsh stretch of confinement with hard labor and religious instruction as punishment for the past. This was followed by rehabilitation for the future, by having the convict advance through the stages of the Mark System, where everything he had was bought with his labor and obedience. The third stage of the Mark System was group corrections.

Maconochie wanted to put prisoners in their third stage in groups of six. They would work together and live together. Each man in the group was responsible for the marks of others as well as his own, and if one backslid and lost his marks, all in the group would lose their marks as well. In this way the prisoners would learn mutual dependence and social responsibility. They often worked in groups outside the penal colony, helping settlers build the country. Eventually, one could earn release by having saved a sufficient amount of marks.

Maconochie's grand effort in penal reform was noted in Great Britain and America. However, his efforts were short-lived. By the mid-1800s, colonial indignation put an end to **Transportation**, and the decreasing need for convict laborers by settlers diminished. By 1845, Maconochie was recalled to England, and management of the penal colony returned to the old ways of confinement. In Australia, recently, the ACT Prison near Canberra was renamed the Alexander Maconochie Center, in honor of his efforts in reform and humane treatment of prisoners.

The Irish System

The second and a related source of parole is found in the so-called **Irish System**, established by **Sir Walter Crofton**. This included a three-stage treatment program:

> ➤ punishment in solitary confinement for two years
> ➤ congregate labor that included the **Mark System**
> ➤ release on a **ticket-of-leave**.

When an inmate earned release into the community, he had to carry on his person the release ticket and show it to law enforcement on demand. If he was re-arrested, the police would punch a hole in his ticket, nullifying the release. The reader might have heard of the expression, "I'm going to punch your ticket," meaning you're out, or you're through. Well, just like most expressions, this one was based on a practice.

The Indeterminate Sentence

Experiments in various forms of early release from prison spread around Europe and to America. The most noted one in America occurred at Elmira Reformatory in 1876, under Brockway, as described in Chapter 4. He introduced the indeterminate sentence and parole as reform elements in the prison experience. A research report of 1888 showed that 78.5

percent of the 1,125 inmates paroled to date became self-supporting, stable, and did not re-offend. This meant that the recidivist rate, rate of re-offending, was 21.5 percent. This recidivist rate has ever after been used as a measure of parole's success.

By the early 1900s, a majority of states had introduced the indeterminate sentence and assumed rehabilitation as a goal. In California, parole for adults was introduced in 1917, when the Legislature enacted the indeterminate sentence law. Juvenile parole began when the California Youth Authority was established in 1941.

The Board of Parole Hearings

When initially created, the adult parole board was a 7-member board, known as the Adult Authority. The name was later changed to the Community Release Board. In 1977, when the purpose of prison became punishment instead of rehabilitation, the name of the Board was changed to The Board of Prison Terms. Also, there was a Woman's Board of Terms and Parole but several years ago that was combined with the existing men's board. The juvenile parole board was called the Youth Offender Parole Board.

Effective July 1, 2005, California's Department of Corrections was reorganized to add the term *Rehabilitation,* to again reflect a focus on rehabilitation. As previously noted, within CDCR is the Division of Adult Institutions and the Division of Juvenile Facilities. Along with this change, the Board of Prison Terms and the Youthful Offender Board were abolished, and a new board, the **Board of Parole Hearings (BPH),** was created.

The Board is comprised of seventeen members called commissioners, appointed by the Governor and confirmed by the Senate. Twelve commissioners hear adult parole matters and five commissioners hear juvenile parole cases. They receive a current annual salary of $99,639. Each board member is appointed by the Governor to a 4-year term and these terms are staggered and do not all coincide with any one Governor's term.

Adult Parole

Adult Parole in California is defined as:

> **the conditional and revocable release of a prison inmate into the community, after serving some portion of a prison sentence, under the supervision of a parole agent.**

As of January 31, 2007, there were approximately 123,046 offenders on parole in California, ninety percent of whom were paroled to their county of last legal residence.

Roles of the Board of Parole Hearings

The BPH has several responsibilities to fulfill within adult corrections.

- ➢ grant parole for ISL inmates

- ➢ set the conditions that all parolees must follow

- ➢ may waive any parole requirements and release the offender from its jurisdiction

- ➢ conducts certification, placement, and parole revocation hearings for mentally disordered sex offenders (MDSO)

- ➢ at the request of the Governor, investigates and makes recommendations on all applications for reprieves, pardons, and commutations of sentence, including death penalty commutations

- ➢ considers requests from foreign born inmates who wish to transfer to their native country to serve their sentences

- ➢ reviews the sentence of each inmate and can refer a case back to the sentencing judge with a recommendation that the judge re-sentence the offender

- ➢ investigates inmate claims of innocence, mitigating factors not considered at sentencing, requests for medical release, and evidence of Battered Women's Syndrome

The Parole Process

The BPH considers parole release and establishes the terms and conditions of parole for all persons sentenced in California under the **Indeterminate Sentence Law**.

Anyone sentenced to prison with a maximum term of life, may be on parole, if parole is granted, for the remainder of his or her life. Any revocation of parole means that the person will continue serving the life sentence, with any subsequent release on parole made at the discretion of the Board.

An ISL inmate may initially be considered after he or she has served the minimum eligibility time, as stated in the Penal Code. Thereafter, the inmate may appear before the Board every year or two, depending upon the offense, for parole consideration. Parole will be granted when the Board believes that the inmate has made the necessary progress toward rehabilitation and does not pose a threat to society. Parole in these cases is **discretionary release**; release at the discretion of the Board.

Anyone sentenced to prison for any non-life felony, other than those defined as violent felonies, will be on parole for three years, which can be extended for one year for good cause. Anyone sentenced for a violent felony, as defined in §667.5 PC, will be on parole for five years. In fact, the sentencing judge must inform a defendant of these time requirements whenever the conviction is obtained by a guilty plea.

As mentioned in a previous discussion of the DSL, parole is automatic after the inmate serves the time given, less any good time or work time credits. Parole cannot be denied by any authority. The parole of all inmates sentenced under the DSL is called **mandatory release**, because their parole is mandatory. The BPH cannot deny parole.

An **inmate cannot refuse parole**. This poses a problem both for public safety and for the parolee trying to succeed if he or she has served many years isolated in a SHU. Trying to re-adjust back into society is a particular problem, and approximately 70 percent of the parolees are returned to prison as parole violators. Ask yourself: is this any way to run a railroad?

Shortly before the inmates scheduled parole hearing date, an institutional parole agent completes an investigation and report to the Board, summarizing the background of the parolee and the offense, and the resources available within the jurisdiction into which the parolee will be released, and recommends a **parole plan** with the appropriate conditions.

Sample Parole Contract

NOTICE OF CONDITIONS OF PAROLE (CDCR # 1515)

You will be released on parole effective _____, 2007, for a period of _____. This parole is subject to the following notice and conditions. Should you violate conditions of this parole, you are subject to arrest, suspension, and/or revocation of your parole.

You waive extradition to the State of California from any state or territory of the US or the District of Columbia. You will not contest any effort to return you to the state of California.

When the Board of Parole Hearings determines, based upon psychiatric reasons, that you are a danger to yourself or others, the Board may, if necessary for psychiatric treatment, order placement in a community treatment facility or state prison or may revoke your parole and order your return to prison.

You and your residence and any property under your control may be searched without a warrant by any agent of CDCR or any law enforcement officer.

If another jurisdiction has lodged a detainer against you, you may be released to the custody of that jurisdiction. Should you not be released from their custody prior to the expiration of your California parole, or should the detainer not be exercised, you are to immediately contact the nearest CDCR parole office for instructions concerning reporting to a parole agent.

You have been informed and have received a copy in writing of the procedure for obtaining a Certificate of Rehabilitation (§4852.21 PC).

Conditions of Parole

1.SPECIAL CONDITIONS: (a) must relate to the crime for which you were convicted; (b) relate to conduct which is itself criminal; (c) prohibit conduct which may be related to future criminality. You are subject to the following special conditions:_____(see below)_____.

Reasons for imposing special conditions:_____.

2.RELEASE, REPORTING, RESIDENCE, AND TRAVEL: Unless other arrangements are approved in writing, you will report to your parole agent on the first working day following your release. Any change of residence shall be reported to your parole agent in advance. You will inform your parole agent within 72 hours of any change of employment location, employer, or termination of employment.

3.PAROLE AGENT INSTRUCTIONS: You shall comply with all instructions of your parole agent and will not travel more than 50 miles from your residence without

---

4.CRIMINAL CONDUCT: Your shall not engage in conduct prohibited by law. You shall immediately inform your parole agent if you are arrested. Conduct prohibited by law might result in parole violation even though no criminal conviction occurs.

5.WEAPONS: You shall not own, use, or have access to, or have under your control: (a) any type of firearm or instrument or device which a reasonable person would believe to be capable of being used as a firearm or any ammunition which could be used in a firearm; (b) any weapon as defined in state or federal statutes or listed in California §12020 PC or any instrument or device which a reasonable person would believe to be capable of being used as a weapon as so defined; (c) any knife with a blade longer than two inches, except kitchen knives which must be kept in your residence and knives related to your employment which may be used and carried only in connection with your employment; or (d) a crowbar of any kind.

6. You shall sign this parole agreement containing the conditions of parole specified in the BPH Rules and any special conditions imposed as specified in the rules. Penal Code Section 3060.5 provides that the BPH shall revoke the parole of any prisoner/parolee who refuses to sign this Notice Of Conditions of Parole. You have the right to appeal the special conditions of parole. Special conditions imposed by the BPH may be appealed pursuant to CA Code of Regulations.

I have read or have had read to me and understand the conditions of parole as they apply to me:

CDCR Number   Parolee Name   Parolee Signature

_____

TO BE COMPLETED BY STAFF

Does this inmate/parolee have a qualifying disability requiring effective communication?

In determining where the inmate will be paroled, the original presentence report will be examined for the address given to the probation officer prior to the prison commitment. That will be the county of parole.

If no address is given in the probation report, the original arresting officer's police report will be examined for an address. If no address is listed of record, the inmate will be paroled to the committing county, with a residence to be determined. When paroled, each parolee is given $200.00 **gate money,** and may be eligible for additional emergency funds.

When a felon is paroled, the Board of Parole Hearings will set the parole conditions, which are **standard conditions,** those required of all parolees, and **special conditions**, those unique to the parolee's offense and background, **and supervision needs.**

Special conditions are selected from the list below and added to the parole contract. Note that a 3-way search clause is a standard condition of all parolees and it will be the condition most frequently enforced, particularly when the parolee is suspected of drug or gang activities.

Department of Corrections and Rehabilitation
Parole and Community Services Division

SPECIAL CONDITIONS OF PAROLE

1. You will participate in ant1-narcotic testing as directed by your Parole Agent.
2. You will not possess or consume alcohol and you will submit to alcohol testing.
3. You will attend the Parole Outpatient Clinic for an evaluation or treatment as directed.
4. You will not have any contact with the victim of your commitment offense or any member of the victim's family.
5. You must have all employment approved by your Parole Agent in advance of accepting the job.
6. You will participate in drug treatment as directed by your Parole Agent or the Board of Parole Hearings.
7. You are prohibited from residing in a Single Family Dwelling with another 290 PC Registrant, unless you are legally related by blood, marriage or adoption.
8. You are prohibited from residing within one-quarter mile of any school that contains Kindergarten through Twelfth grades.
9. You will not have contact with minors in any manner (in person, by telephone, by mail, by computer or through a third party) without the prior written approval of your Parole Agent.
10. You are not to possess or operate a computer without the prior written approval of your Parole Agent.
11. You shall not contact or associate with any person you know or reasonably should have known to be a gang member or associate.
12. You are not to wear, or have in your possession, clothing/apparel with colors you know or should have known to be affiliated with a gang.
13. You are not to possess items such as photographs, written material, publications, jewelry, or any other items depicting/describing activity/association you know or should have known were gang related.
14. You will enroll in and successfully complete a Batterers Program as outlined in Penal Code Section 1203.97

Signature:_____

The 24/7 3-way search clause orders the parolee to submit to search by any peace officer at any time. Consequently, any law enforcement officer may stop and search a parolee provided that the **officer knows in advance** of the search clause.

Special conditions of parole are included in an addendum to this notice of conditions. They must relate to the crime or potential criminality. Those that are appropriate to any given parolee are selected from the list below.

If a parolee refuses to accept his or her parole conditions and will not sign the parole order, parole is immediately revoked and the offender is returned to prison.

Parole Revocation Procedures

Approximately fifty percent of the felons released on parole are returned to prison on a technical parole violation, and approximately twenty percent return for new crimes. A parolee may violate his or her parole by either committing a new offense or by breaking one of the conditions of parole, a technical violation. Since a 1972 U. S. Supreme Court decision (*Morrissey v. Brewer*, **1972**), parole revocation cases require a two-stage hearing process.

The first stage is actually called a **Morrissey Hearing**, and is a probable cause hearing before a representative of the BPH in which the parole agent must establish **probable cause** to believe that a violation occurred. The second stage is the actual **violation hearing** and is similar to a trial, only without a jury and before a BPH commissioner or panel of three commissioners. There has been on-going civil litigation since 1994 over whether the revocation procedures actually violated a parolee's due process. The matter was settled by both sides and a settlement agreement reached in 2005, implementing speedy due process procedures (*Valdivia v. Schwarzenegger*, 2005). Every parolee will be appointed an attorney when a violation has been alleged and the attorney has the right to discovery, to cross-examine witnesses against his or her client, and to present witnesses on his or her client's behalf. The Board must state its reason for revoking parole, with its decision based on a preponderance of the evidence.

If the Board revokes parole, the parolee may be returned to prison for up to one year. There is a shortcut to this formal revocation process. If the parolee might be offered a plea-bargain, as it were, to admit the violation for a guaranteed consequence, the case is referred to what is termed a **Valdivia attorney** from CDCR, who examines the case and may proceed with "Let's Make a Deal."

For example, a parolee might be willing to admit a violation if he or she is guaranteed a three month placement in a drug rehabilitation program rather than going through the formal process, with the possibility of receiving another year back in prison.

Effects of AB 109 on Parole

Now after understanding the parole process described above, we need to re-consider how parole will operate under AB 109.

Post-Release (County-Level) Community Supervision

CDCR continues to have jurisdiction over all offenders who are on state parole prior to the implementation date of October 1, 2011. Prospectively, county-level supervision for offenders upon release from prison will include current non-violent, current non-serious (irrespective of priors), and some sex offenders. County-level supervision will <u>not</u> include:

- Inmates paroled from life terms to include third-strike offenders

- Offenders whose current commitment offense is violent or serious, as defined by California's Penal Code §§ 667.5(c) and 1192.7(c)

- High-risk sex offenders, as defined by CDCR

- Mentally Disordered Offenders

- Offenders on parole prior to October 1, 2011

Offenders who meet the above-stated conditions will continue to be under state parole supervision.

Parole Revocations

Parolees who violate after September 30, 2011, will serve their revocation time in county jail instead of prison and it can only be up to 180 days. **No person shall be returned to prison** on a parole revocation except for those life-term offenders who paroled pursuant to Penal Code §3000.1 (Penal Code §3056 states that only these offenders may be returned to state prison).

The responsibility of parole revocations for inmates released to county supervision shall be with the local courts. The responsibility of parole revocations for inmates released to the Division of Adult Operations' supervision will continue under the Board of Parole Hearings until July 1, 2013, at which time the entire parole revocation process shall be a local court-based process. On July 1, 2013, the local courts will become the sole parole authority. Contracting back to the state for offenders to complete a period of parole revocation is not an option. Only life term offenders who paroled pursuant to PC section 3000.1 can be returned to state prison.

After July, 1, 2013 The Board of Parole Hearings will continue to conduct:
- Parole consideration for lifers
- Medical parole hearings
- Mentally disordered offender cases
- Sexually Violent Predator cases

Public Safety Realignment also provides the following under parole:
- Allows local parole revocations up to 180 days
- Authorizes flash incarceration at the local level for up to 10 days

Life term inmates paroled pursuant to PC section 3000.1 (e.g., murderers, specific life term sex offenses) will be eligible for return back to state prison if parole is revoked for 30 days or more.

The Division of Juvenile Justice AB 109 limited the future juvenile court commitments to the Division of Juvenile Justice (DJJ). However, AB 117 removes this provision. As such, there will be no changes to DJJ during the 2011 realignment.

Parole Supervision

The parole agent is an agent of the **executive branch** of state government, as opposed to a probation officer, who is under the judicial branch of government. A parole agent has peace officer powers that are limited to his or her occupational needs and conditions. Parole agents hired after January 1, 1988 must complete and qualify in firearms training and will be armed on the job. Those hired before 1988 may choose not to be armed.

Parolees are classified as to the level of supervision required. So-called **high control parolees** must report within 24 hours of release, or on the next business day following release. **Regular supervision parolees** may report within 72 hours. The initial interview between all parolees and their parole agents clarifies the parole conditions and expectations the parolee must meet. He or she is photographed, along with any unusual marks or tattoos. This information is immediately entered into a statewide identification system (LEADS) for the purposes of matching it with a description of any wanted person. Usually, a DNA sample has already been obtained at the prison.

High control parolees receive an initial home visit from the agent within three days, and thereafter twice a month, plus collateral contacts. Regular supervision parolees receive an initial home visit within ten days, and thereafter at least three times per quarter. Most agents make more frequent contacts and spend as much time as possible in the field. Parolees do make office visits as well, but the agent only learns what the parolee wants to tell during an office visit. The agent can learn much more about the parolee's life style from home visits and collateral contact.

Honorable Discharge

A parolee who completes parole is given an **honorable discharge** by the BPH. He or she may thereafter apply to the committing court for a Certificate of Rehabilitation, which restores certain rights to the parolee.

He or she may also apply to the Board of Parole Hearings for consideration to receive a pardon from the Governor. Regular supervision parolees are advised during their initial parole interview that if they complete thirteen months of parole without a violation, they may be discharged from parole directly by the parole unit supervisor.

This might act as an incentive to a motivated parolee to keep clean for thirteen months, with early termination as a reward.

Restoration of Rights for a Convicted Felon

In California, the granting of a Certificate of Rehabilitation (CR) or a Governor's pardon restores to the applicant some rights of citizenship that were forfeited as a result of a felony conviction. A Certificate of Rehabilitation is granted by the court of origin. The following briefly summarizes what each does and does not restore.

Certificate of Rehabilitation

A certificate:

DOES:

➢ relieve <u>some</u> sex offenders, as specified, of further duty to register. (§290.5 PC.)

➢ enhance a felon's potential for licensing consideration by a State board. (§4853 PC.)

➢ serve as an official document to demonstrate a felon's rehabilitation, which could enhance employment possibilities.

➢ serve as an automatic application for a gubernatorial pardon.

DOES NOT:

➢ erase the felony conviction or seal the criminal record. (§4852.17 PC.)

➢ prevent the offense from being considered as a prior conviction if the person is later convicted of a new offense.

➢ allow a felon to answer on employment applications that he or she has no record of conviction.

➢ give a felon the right to vote - this right is automatically restored after termination from probation or discharge from parole.

Pardon

A pardon is granted by the Governor, after an investigation and recommendation by the BPH. A pardon:

DOES:

➢ allow a felon to serve on a jury trial. (Code Civ. Proc. §203 subd. (a)(5).)

➢ allow restoration of firearms rights, upon federal approval, to specified offenders if granted a full and unconditional pardon, *unless* the conviction was for a felony involving the use of a dangerous weapon. (§4854 PC)

➢   allow a felon to be considered for appointment as a county probation officer or a state parole agent, but not to any other peace officer positions. (Gov. Code § 1029.)

➢   allow specified sex offenders still required to register after obtaining a CR to be relieved of duty to register if granted a full pardon. (§290.5 PC)

DOES NOT:

➢   erase the felony conviction or seal the criminal record. (§4852.17 PC.)

➢   prevent the offense from being considered as a prior conviction if the person is later convicted of a new offense.

➢   allow a felon to answer on employment applications that he or she has or record of conviction.

Juvenile Parole

The Board of Parole Hearings Authority

Although considered a parole board, the range of the Board's authority over what happens to a juvenile committed to DJF is far more comprehensive than that implied in the mere name *parole*. Their control was almost total. In this area of examination it operates far differently than the parole board members hearing adult cases.

Before 2011, when a minor was committed to DJF, the Board had the authority to:

> ➢ accept or reject the minor and may return him or her to court
> ➢ determine the length of confinement
> ➢ order the place of confinement
> ➢ order the type of programming for each minor
> ➢ determine how often a minor will appear before the Board for parole consideration, and when the minor is actually ready for release
> ➢ order parole

> ➤ set parole conditions
> ➤ revoke or modify parole
> ➤ discharge a juvenile parolee from parole

As of 2011, items 6 through 9, listed above, are no longer within the scope of the Board's authority. This is a significant change made by realignment legislation in the field of juvenile justice. The year 2011 will become the benchmark used to measure the rise and demise of DJJ and DJF.

Juveniles committed are sent to a reception center for examination, evaluation, and determination as to program needs. If the Board thinks that the minor cannot benefit from a DJF program, the Board can refuse to accept the commitment and return the minor to the court for another disposition. The Board can also refuse anyone with a communicable disease, or one whose behavior would be disruptive to a DJF program. If the Board accepts the commitment, it sets a **confinement time and parole consideration date (PCD)** for the minor, usually within one or two years of reception.

Programming and Review

After the juvenile's PCD has been determined, the Board decides in which institution the minor will **program**, and in what program the juvenile will participate, ie., school, vocational training, or a forestry camp.

The progress of each ward is reviewed annually by a 3-member Panel Board to determine how the minor is programming and/or if the initial time set by the Board should be modified with a new PCD. The Panel Board may alter the time set by up to six months. If the case is referred up to a Full Board *en banc*, it has no limit on how much it may alter the amount of time. It may parole immediately or detain until the maximum confinement time given by the committing judge is served.

When a ward completes his or her **Board-ordered confinement time,** he or she appears before a Full Board, who meets at the institution to determine if the minor is ready for parole. The Board may deny parole and continue the case for up to one year, with a new PCD. The Board may continue a case like this for good cause, denying parole until the juvenile either serves all of the maximum confinement time given by the judge, or reaches the age at which jurisdiction terminates.

Rarely does a juvenile serve his or her entire maximum confinement time. Usually the Board grants parole when and if a ward satisfactorily completes the Board's ordered time and program.

Division of Juvenile Parole Operations

Parole services are operated by the **Division of Juvenile Parole Operations (DJPO)** which makes them agents of the executive branch of government. Parole agents work within this division. However, they also are accountable to the Board of Parole Hearings for the supervision provided parolees, and they are the enforcement arm of the state parole system to make sure the parolees obey the conditions.

Parole Consideration

Juvenile parole, as we know it, is now a misnomer (AB 1628). Aftercare, once known as parole, is now called **post-release** and will be performed by the county probation departments. Effective January 17, 2011, the Juvenile Parole Board is no longer authorized to release wards on parole. Instead, the Board will refer the cases of juveniles ready for **discharge** from DJF to the committing court, 60 days prior to the release date, along with the Board's post-release recommendations as to what conditions it suggests for effective supervision. The committing court will schedule a **re-entry dispositional hearing** and will refer the case to the probation investigation unit to prepare a court report as to the appropriate supervision terms and conditions. The juvenile will subsequently be placed on probation. However, the parole process is still in a state of flux, and parole offices are, as of March 2011, still receiving wards on their caseloads, and they have a number of parolees currently on parole supervision.

Nevertheless, as stated in §1766 PC and AB 1628, as of July 1, 2014, all juvenile parolees will be transferred to the committing juvenile court jurisdictions for probation supervision. This, of course, implies that there will still be juveniles on parole by that time. In reality, most all juvenile parolees today are between the ages of 18 and 25, and will be handled as adult offenders for any new crimes. Also, a majority of them have already used all their commitment time, so if they violate parole, there will not be any additional time to serve as a consequence. The worst case scenario for them would be a dishonorable discharge.

The new release and discharge to probation supervision is detailed in Section 1768.01 WIC. It requires DJF, at least 60 days before a ward's scheduled discharge consideration hearing before the Board, to provide the original committing court and the probation department with the most recent written case review, as well as notice of the discharge consideration hearing date.

At the discharge consideration hearing, the Board considers everything documented in the minor's file, to include school or vocational trade reports, behavior, staff reports, and any diagnostic reports that might be available. This information usually is provided in a cumulative report, prepared by an institutional parole agent or counselor. If all is favorable, a release and discharge to probation supervision date is scheduled for the juvenile. The Board then must send its post-release recommendations about the juvenile's supervision needs to the court, within seven days, and set a specific release date at least fourteen days after that determination.

Section 1766.01(c)(6) WIC requires the committing court to hold a re-entry disposition hearing to determine and set the appropriate terms and conditions for the juvenile's probation supervision. The court will include any recommendations by the Board that the court deems appropriate for the best interests of the minor and the public safety.

Since there are only about 1,000 juvenile court ward commitments in DJF at this time, their releases to the various counties will probably have a minimum impact on their resources. Those juveniles placed on post release supervision will be ordered to comply with certain conditions.

> **standard**, those required of all parolees

> **special**, those imposed individually on a particular case

A majority of parolees are ordered to submit to chemical testing, because drugs are such a part of today's juvenile scene. All parolees must agree to a 24/7 3-way search and other conditions listed in the parole contract. This is a binding contract that the parolee reads and signs before release.

Parole Supervision

Traditional juvenile parole is defined as:

the conditional, revocable, and supervised release of a ward from a DJF institution after serving some portion of his or her maximum confinement time.

Post release supervision by a probation officer fits within this same definition. Two aspects of post release supervision need discussion:

> the intensity of the supervision once parole supervision has begun

> the time span between the ward's commitment and initial parole agent contact

Both depend on the type of programming in which a ward has been involved in the institution, and the length of his or her confinement time.

Parole Agent's Authority

There will continue to be juvenile parole agents until sometime in 2014, at which time the state's juvenile justice system is to be no longer. Parole agents derive their authority from Section 830.5 of the Penal Code. They have peace officer status 24 hours a day, but peace officer authority only when they are in the performance of their regular job. Any parole agent hired after 1977, must be armed while on duty.

Those hired before 1977 may be armed if they choose to. This is still a sensitive issue. Some do not want to carry a gun. They became parole agents from the social worker perspective and do not want to be a *cop*. Other agents feel the opposite, and would not work without being armed. In either case, the parole agent plays the **dual role** of helper and enforcer, just as was described for a probation officer. However, the type of offender on parole usually is more mature and delinquently oriented than are many of the probationers.

Levels of Supervision

The size of each caseload usually reflects the intensity of supervision required. A field parole agent, the one who will be supervising the ward on parole, probably will have contact with the case during the last sixty to ninety days of the minor's confinement time. When the ward is paroled, the initial supervision will be very intense. The intensity, or frequency of contacts, will decrease after the first ninety days of parole, then even less after about six months, if all is going well.

Intensity is equated with frequency of contact. Most parole agents are **generalists**, supervising whoever lives within their assigned geographic area. The so-called **regular supervision** case is ideally 70 wards, however, they might be higher, and specialized caseloads might be less. **Specialized caseloads** provide intensive services for such offenders as sex offenders, drug offenders, those needing special placement, those having mental problems, and those whose history shows heavy involvement with gang activities. Electronic or GPS monitoring is a condition of most intensive cases.

Parole Success or Failure

A juvenile can remain on parole until the end of the state's jurisdiction, which is age 25, or until he or she is given a discharge by the Board. If all goes well on parole, the juvenile can receive an **Honorable Discharge** after twelve to eighteen months, depending on the committing offense. An actual discharge hearing is conducted, but the minor need not attend. He or she may attend, and some do, just to brag about their success and to receive accolades from the Board. The promise of an Honorable Discharge should provide strong motivation for a parolee. As the code states:

Release of honorably discharged persons carries release from all penalties....All persons honorably discharged from control of the Youth Authority Board shall thereafter be released from all penalties or disabilities resulting from the offenses for which they were committed, including, but not limited, to, any disqualification for any employment or occupational license, or both, created by any other provision of law. However, such a person shall not be eligible for appointment as a peace officer employed by any public agency if his or her appointment would otherwise be prohibited by Section 1029 of the Government Code.

Unfortunately, many juveniles do not receive an Honorable Discharge. They are over age 18 when paroled, and if they re-offend, are arrested as an adult, and are processed through the adult system. Consequently, they are given either a General or Dishonorable Discharge and parole is terminated due to loss of jurisdiction.

If a juvenile does complete parole honorably, he or she may petition the original court to have the records sealed after six years have elapsed from the date of discharge. If the successful juvenile parolee has an adult criminal court commitment to DJF, he or she may petition the court to reverse the original conviction and dismiss the charges. In either event, he or she will not have a criminal conviction.

If a parolee can remain crime free and violation free for the first ninety to one hundred-twenty days, he or she has a very good chance of succeeding on parole. The parole agent is there to help in any way possible, but the responsibility to make it lies with the parolee. Many do succeed, and go on to lead productive and crime-free lives, receiving an **Honorable Discharge** and a dismissal of the charges by the committing court. A vast majority do not succeed and are returned to custody on parole violations.

A parolee, like a probationer, may commit either a **technical violation**, such as failing to report, absconding from supervision, or receiving a positive drug test, or may violate parole by committing a **new offense**.

Technical violations and new petty offenses may be handled at the unit supervisor level, if the parolee admits the violation or does not contest it and agrees to accept the proposed disposition. The supervisor may take what is termed a **Corrective Action Plan**, modifying parole conditions to add short term treatment. This often includes placement in a drug rehabilitation facility, a commonly used disposition.

Serious law violators are referred to the Board for disposition. Unless the ward admits the violation or does not contest it and agrees to the proposed revocation time, the case will follow the same formal procedures as would an adult case. This includes a *Morrissey Hearing* and a **violation hearing**, and the parolee is entitled to full due process. Because of a civil suit related to the *Valdivia* case referred to above, this process is expedited and follows all the due process guarantees.

If parole is revoked, the ward is returned to an institution and is assigned to some sort of program, with a new PCD. A short-term return for drug re-hab could be from thirty to ninety days. A full program could be for a year or eighteen months. The parolee may be returned for the remainder of his or her maximum confinement time.

Summary

This chapter presented the elements of state parole in two sections, adult parole and juvenile parole. It was noted that since 2005, CDCR is the umbrella agency under which operates a single state parole board, the Board of Parole Hearings. Seventeen commissioners, aided by civil service assistant commissioners, divide their duties so that twelve hear adult cases and five hear juvenile cases.

Parole conditions and supervision in both adult and juvenile cases were reviewed, along with the successful completion of parole leading to an honorable discharge. Within a given time after discharge, an adult parolee may apply for a Certificate of Rehabilitation with the sentencing court, then apply for a pardon from the Governor. After a juvenile completes parole, he or she may petition the juvenile court to set aside the original findings (verdict) and dismiss the petition.

In the months and years to come, the youth offender will become and remain the responsibility of local jurisdictions and will be supervised by county probation officers. Juvenile court and probation procedures will apply and the section above on juvenile parole will be relegated to the history portion of the book's next edition. Violent and serious youth offenders will find themselves in adult court and adult institutions.

References

Norval, Morris. *Maconochie's Gentlemen: The Story of Norfolk Island and the Roots of Modern Prison Reform (Studies in Crime and Public Policy).* New York: Oxford University Press, 2002

Peoples, Edward E. *Criminal Procedures in California, 3rd ed.* Forestville: Meadow Crest Publishing, 2006.

Peoples, Edward E. *Juvenile Procedures in California, 4th ed.* Forestville: Meadow Crest Publishing, 2006.

Internet References

http://www.cs.act.gov.au/amc/home/ambiography
http://www.irishprisons.ie/history.asp

Case Decisions

Morrissey v. Brewer, 408 U.S. 481

Subject Index

Case Index

Photo Index

Made in the USA
San Bernardino, CA
28 January 2018